the other side of empathy

the
other
side of
empathy

JADE E. DAVIS

DUKE UNIVERSITY PRESS
Durham and London
2023

© 2023 DUKE UNIVERSITY PRESS
All rights reserved
Project editor: Bird Williams
Designed by A. Mattson Gallagher
Typeset in Minion Pro and General Sans
by Westchester Publishing Services

Library of Congress Cataloging-in-Publication Data Names:
Davis, Jade E., author.
Title: The other side of empathy / Jade E. Davis. Description:
Durham : Duke University Press, 2023. |
Includes bibliographical references and index.
Identifiers: LCCN 2022048185 (print)
LCCN 2022048186 (ebook)
ISBN 9781478025016 (paperback)
ISBN 9781478020035 (hardcover)
ISBN 9781478027010 (ebook)
Subjects: LCSH: Empathy. | Other (Philosophy)—
Social aspects. | Human zoos—History—19th century. |
Photography—Social aspects—History—19th century. |
Racism in anthropology—History. | Colonization—Social
aspects. | Technology—Social aspects. | BISAC: SOCIAL
SCIENCE / Ethnic Studies / American / African American &
Black Studies
Classification: LCC BF 575. E55 D36 2023 (print)
LCC BF575. E55 (ebook)
DCC 152.4/1—dc23/eng/20230415
LC record available at https://lccn.loc.gov/2022048185
LC ebook record available at https://lccn.loc.gov/2022048186

Cover art: A spectator looking through binoculars at the
Derby horse races, Epsom, Surrey, June 1923. (Photo by
Topical Press Agency/Hulton Archive/Getty Images)

To the women who had names of their own, even if we don't know them today.

Contents

Preface.

I'd like to preface this with . . . I feel you, man.

Because we can never truly know another's feelings or perspective, it is better that we not feel at all. It's better than going down the path of self-actualizing at the cost of temporary self-annihilation coupled with cannibalization that we have come to call "empathy" across all parts of society tasked with cultural reproduction. That is to say, empathy is an illusion at best, or simply—as is said in moments of deep reflection—bullshit!

Here is the list of things I know to be true (not to be confused with Truth) about empathy:

1. Feelings and emotions are chemical pollution of the brain that cloud the accuracy of experience.
2. Reaching radical empathy is to have successfully dehumanized oneself.
3. Empathy leaves the Other stuck in time and place.
4. You are my Other, and I too am yours; this does not mean WE ARE THE SAME.
5. Mediated experiences and the empathy that they *inspire* is an illusion.
6. To be in the shoes of an Other still leaves you with your own feet.
7. Empathy is deployed and used politically as though it were pure transference or communication.

8. Respect, compassion, mutual recognition, and assumptions are better frameworks for understanding.
9. Your irrational feelings are my murder, and you cannot empathize with the dead.
10. The body's empathetic sensations are the body being seduced and overwhelmed by its own feelings.
11. Empathy = DEHUMANIZATION and ALIENATION (first of the Other and then of the Self).

The disenfranchised, the marginalized, and the at-risk are expected to perform their pain and discomfort for those who know only comfort. Those who know only comfort do not realize they sit in a position of privilege and power. Rather than trying to step into the discomfort of others, people should learn to confront, interrogate, and be aware of their own discomfort, preferably with a smile, because empathy is empty.

Empathy Manifesto #3: Kill the body. Leave it behind.
It is forever lost in time.

Empathy is your imagined present and the future made up of the past. Feelings displaced corporeally and temporally temporarily reduce the ones living to anchors for their feelings about a fabricated past we call "History." This is domination by agents of oppression and interpreted by those attempting to absolve themselves of guilt. Their word for freedom to do as they please is EMPATHY, the evil eraser. The dead and silent of us create an archive for them. An archive of those who can't tell them, "You are out of line." And of those who are not invited to speak when all they want to say is: "I am human. I am human. I am human!"

A call met with calls for silence, a cultural shushing, so others can make sure the time we are lost to is a time of suffering.

For the anger that can't be contained
and the feelings that are often left out of words.
For the dead who cannot speak now and whose words were lost in the past,
this is a call to feminism, the decolonial, Blackness, and invisibility.
This is a call to a political practice in a time of crisis that is now generations old.
This is a rejection of the postcolonial.

There is a call to decolonize *your* version of the past.

STOP TRYING TO COMPRESS TIME SO YOU CAN GET LOST IN YOUR
FEELINGS.

Acknowledgments.

Foremost, I would like to express my sincere gratitude to Cathy N. Davidson and Ken Hillis for their continuous support, patience, motivation, and enthusiasm as I've sorted through my thoughts over the last decade. I hope to be able to make time, support, and be excited for others who are curious and know only how to think sideways, as they did for me.

I am forever indebted to Nicky Agate for reviewing my translations and helping to ensure I was capturing what was being said in the language of the past as *divertissement* and not work. I would have been lost without you.

I would also like to thank Demetrios Kapatenakos, for always being a phone call away when I had a random thought; Jordan Davis, for coming along for the ride; Patricia Matthew and Melissa Creary, for constant encouragement; Jackie Cahill and Jon Shaw.

I would like to thank and send all my love to Justin M., for creating space and time for me to think; Tristan and Donovan M., for keeping me focused on what's important (it's both of you); and Lucille Howard Brantley Russell, my grandma, for always telling me my job was to do more than she was allowed to do, on my own terms, and for always being interested in what I was up to, even if she never saw the point (though she did love looking at photographs with me).

And to all of those whom I encounter digitally and who inspire me, make me curious, or help me discover new worlds that I will never meet because of the distance of time, place, and circumstance.

By way of an introduction.

If good emotions are cultivated, and are worked on and towards, then they remain defined against uncultivated or unruly emotions, which frustrate the formation of the competent self. Those who are "other" to me or us, or those that threaten to make us other, remain the source of bad feeling in this model of emotional intelligence.
—Sara Ahmed, *The Cultural Politics of Emotion*

Empathy is an expression of the colonization of psychic space.

This book is a critique of empathy culture, not the ideals behind empathy. By empathy culture, I mean the current cultural narrative in which a lack of empathy is used for all forms of disavowal: the goodness or worthiness of people, humanness of the self and others, or any degree of compassion and caring. I mean the culture where empathy is lobbied, uncritically, as a solution to techno-determinism, medical malpractice, racism, inequality, war, and all other ills plaguing humanity. I mean the culture of workshops, self-help books, TED talks, and lesson plans to make everyone more empathetic without doing the work of modeling goodness, humanness, compassion, or caring. Empathy is a quick fix for a broken culture, and like most quick fixes, it is prone to distortion, peeling away, not quite fitting, or failing altogether. Empathy is a binary. You either have it, or you don't. And if you aren't empathetic, you are a lost cause. The altruistic impulse, the ability to function in society, to make a living, work in a team, lead people, follow people, not kill, and every other matter of being today is dependent on empathy.

Change and action stop being necessary in empathy culture because the feeling and sense of understanding are action enough. In empathy culture, understanding and care for the Other requires personal empathy, a process by which, in theory, one completely gives the self to the idea of the Other as though that idea were the actual other person. In this process, the empathizer temporarily must lose the self in order to care for the Other. There is no space for structural change, discussions of biases, or imagining reality otherwise as a collective. Everything is done at the level of the individual and is based on individual emotional connection, maturity, and perspectives. That is to say, empathy culture deploys empathy as a cure for structural issues without critically engaging its limits or allowing for other means of affective engagement. It asks, at an individual level, that we use a technique of colonization and allow the Other to have a seat in our psychic space so we can, in turn, use the perceived firsthand knowledge that we gain psychically to create a narrative.

My argument on the necessity of forfeiting empathy on the road to decolonization is informed primarily by the monumental thinking of political philosopher and psychiatrist Frantz Fanon. In line with Fanon's work, the work of culture and the dominant gaze cannot be separated. Before I discuss the empathetic gaze, though, I would like to discuss "empathy." When these narratives are fed collectively through ideological structures, the limits of individual culture are shifted back to the collective understanding of the dominant culture.

Empathy is a relatively new concept. It entered the English lexicon in 1909 as a translation by the British psychologist Edward Bradford Titchener from the German word *Einfühlung*, itself an invented term with origins in German phenomenology and German aesthetics of the late eighteenth and early nineteenth centuries. *Einfühlung* is often translated as "in feeling" or "feeling into." From there, the concept can be traced through various philosophers and aestheticians until it is adopted as a foundational concept in modern social science.[1] The more modern use of the concept of empathy can be traced to philosopher David Hume who had the insight that "the minds of men are mirrors to one another, not only because they reflect each other's emotions, but also because those rays of passions, sentiments and opinions may be often reverberated, and may decay away by insensible degrees."[2] He was, of course, speaking of sympathy, understood by Hume as the "communication of sentiments from one thinking being to another."[3] I do not think it is a coincidence that this appeared in a section titled "Of Our Esteem for the Rich and Powerful."[4] In empathy culture, sympathy has been replaced by and is still riddled with power dynamics based on the cultural esteem given to the rich and powerful.

For the purposes of this project, the empathy being discussed is the empathy that reemerged of empathy in the 1960s, when it becomes tightly bound with ideas of altruism and colonialism.[5] Interestingly, definitions and discussions of empathy in the 1960s often separated feelings from the mindset of an Other, as highlighted in "Development of an Empathy Scale" by Robert Hogan: "The consensus of dictionaries is that empathy means the intellectual or imaginative apprehension of another's condition or state of mind without actually experiencing that person's feelings."[6] Empathy culture lost this part; or rather, it has conflated what "I" feel with the feelings of another. Objectification is central to the concept of empathy and linked to its roots in aesthetic theory. Over time, as the objects of empathy became people, the focus shifted to emotions and feelings.

Recent definitions of empathy have reflected this shift by acknowledging that the roots of the word involve taking on mental states; but the current meaning ends up being situated in the philosophy of emotions. The philosopher I find myself turning to when I need a definition is the British philosopher of aesthetics and ethics Derek Matravers, the author of such books as *Art and Emotion* (1998) and *Empathy* (2017):

> Empathy at least involves this: imagining oneself (whether consciously or unconsciously) into another's circumstances and replicating their mental states. For the epistemologists the relevant mental states are cognitive attitudes, and the result is grasping what other people are thinking. For the philosophers of emotion, the moral philosophers, and quite possibly the folk, the relevant mental states are feelings and the result is that one feels what the other person is feeling.[7]

Going from mirroring another's mental state to feeling what a person is feeling is a major shift. Regardless of the realness of empathy, the shift to centering the definition on feelings creates the potential for irrationality to become central to empathy. In my experience, the cultural understanding and use of empathy tends to posit that people are capable of both the epistemological and cognitive aspects of empathy. One can "feel what the other person is feeling"—with a bit of training and practice.

In the essay "These Things Called Empathy: Eight Related but Distinct Phenomena," social psychologist C. Daniel Baston states that empathy is an answer to two questions: "How can one know what another person is thinking and feeling?," and "What leads one person to respond with sensitivity and care to the suffering of another?"[8] Baston's work is important as it eloquently states the risk, or pity, inherent in a feelings-forward version of empathy:

> There is considerable evidence that feeling distress at witnessing another person in distress (concept 7) can produce motivation to help that person. This motivation does not, however, appear to be directed toward the ultimate goal of relieving the other's distress (i.e., altruistic motivation); the motivation appears to be directed toward the ultimate goal of relieving one's own distress (i.e., egoistic motivation; Batson, 1991). As a result, this distress may not lead one to respond with sensitivity to the suffering of another, especially if there is an opportunity to relieve one's own distress without having to relieve the other's distress.[9]

With sympathy, action is the acknowledgment of the Other's suffering, even if the sympathizer is unable to relate to the event that led to the suffering. In contrast, to tend to the self, not before, but above, the Other is related to what counts as action in empathy culture.

The resurgence of empathy and its move into popular culture coincides with the post–World War II world-building of the 1950s and the global social transformation of the 1960s. This period is defined by global civil rights movements, decolonization, the atomic age, the threat of nuclear war, and Western wars in faraway third world countries.[10] The rise of empathy also coincides with an emergent high-definition technology—television—entering homes. All these dynamics created a new sense of proximity across people and places as the world remade itself and people tried to understand each other. The culmination of this can be seen in two studies of humans of the same name through different media. The first was the Museum of Modern Art's 1955 photographic-essay exhibition, "The Family of Man," organized by Edward Steichen. The photo-essay was designed to show universal aspects of the human experience and toured the world for eight years. The exhibition is bookended by John Percival's 1969 seven-episode BBC mini-series of the same name and concept.[11]

The exhibition highlights how distressing experiencing the Other through media can be. By week eleven, a decision was made to remove the photograph of the aftermath of a lynching in Mississippi. This photograph was not included in the exhibition book either. The need to censor material designed to evoke the experience of the Other because it distressed the viewers is an early illustration of some of empathy culture's limits. Today, in the age of reaction videos and gamified experiences, creating distress is often the point. Distress highlights an implicit power differential between the body creating the empathy-enriched experience, the empathizer, and the individual or group who is the subject of the empathizer's gaze. By turning the subject into an object, the subject can be reshaped, discarded, or dismantled. The empathizer can decide an experience is too much and avoid the reality presented to them by walking away. The body/person who created the experience (which is often different from the body/person who had the real-world experience) determines whether the potential encounter with objectified people is "too much." If the discomfort is too much, the experience can be removed altogether.

Empathy culture rewards experiences for producing strong feelings or emotional reactions, the more traumatic or negative the better, to the point of exhaustion or apathy. Striving for the fastest path to a reaction often involves taking shortcuts by leaning into implicit biases. More credit is granted to the empathizer willing to cross interpersonal and interracial divides. When social biases (especially race) are involved, feeling empathy for the Other (without obligating oneself to do anything except express one's empathy) is the easiest form of social credit—and the hollowest. In empathy culture, suffering is central to this system of rewards for feeling and managing distress levels. Suffering is an expected and necessary part of the background of existence and meaning-making. It is always a click away, but it is never supposed to be our own.

The click, the ability to see suffering on demand, makes empathy culture possible by centering the empathetic gaze. Caroline Pedwell, in her article "Theorizing 'African' Female Genital Cutting and 'Western' Body Modifications" states this clearly and highlights the shortcomings of relying on the current forms of empathy popular in Western culture; and in doing so, she provides a meaningful definition of the empathetic gaze:

> In aiding the "western self" to see hidden similarities between herself and the "non-western other," this approach to transnational empathy may collapse into a sameness which, in flattening histories of embodied differentiation, simply reifies the essentialist differences identified as problematic in the first place. Consequently, histories of othering and violence through which particular embodied identities and practices have been (re)constituted are again effaced. At this point we can see how

problematic the erasure of race, cultural difference and nation which I associated with the continuum and analogue approaches above, may be linked to the appropriative construction of the 'western' empathetic gaze.[12]

From this definition, I would like to extract some of the ways in which the empathetic gaze creates harm as a part of empathy culture. This occurs in tandem with Fanon's idea of epidermalization and a cultural drive to reproduce colonization: the empathetic gaze harms because it defines appropriate reactions and understandings of the event or person being seen; the empathetic gaze orients toward the past and is ahistorical; the empathetic gaze reduces a person to an object, denying them their full humanity; the empathetic gaze transforms and consumes suffering as an aesthetic experience; the empathetic gaze comes from a position of power and dominance; and finally, the empathetic gaze uses power and dominance to disassociate suffering of the Other by replacing the distress of the Other with the distress of the self. Without heightened suffering, the empathetic gaze cannot exist.

However, the empathetic gaze avoids direct suffering. Instead, the empathetic gaze desires the end of unmediated cultural guilt for the suffering of others. That is to say, it seeks to mediate all guilt. From my perspective, the goal of a good and universal empathy-based cultural encounter is to not go so far as to cause true distress but, rather, to cause a bit of guilt. The desire of the empathetic gaze is to end guilt when the ability for concern is diminished or impossible due to the distance of time, difference, power, and privilege.[13] Empathy is a cultural tool designed to assuage potential unmediated cultural guilt when the oppression of the past collides with the present, or when people imagined as outside of the present become visible.

New hyperrealist, interactive technologies are offered as a prosthesis, designed to secure and ensure empathy, especially in fraught episodes in which empathy may fray. These often look like colonial struggles and fallout.[14] Virtual reality (and its cinematic counterpart, the 360° video) remains the most prominent technology being used in to envoke empathy, though it is not the only one. The medium has had limited advancement into new forms of experience since its resurgence in 2015, with the emergence of high-end consumer headsets alongside DIY mobile-based solutions like Google Cardboard. An example of how this works is *The Guardian*'s 6 × 9 project, a virtual reality experience in which a viewer can be placed in a 6 × 9 cell and experience what it's like to be in solitary confinement for twenty-three hours a day for weeks, months, or years—in a matter of minutes.[15] The experience is overlaid with six testimonies from disembodied voices of people who were in solitary confinement.

The viewer, limited to a 360° video experience, is asked to understand solitary confinement as torturous and inhumane. But when power and the controlled gaze of the experience come into play, the suggestion is that the person should be doing more to end this experience, and that they are somehow individually responsible for doing something.[16] This leads to guilt. This guilt has no way of being absolved, as it is tied to systems and structures of power and oppression beyond the individual. Empathy is an attempt to erase both one's own culpability and the existence of the Other by making the suffering of the Other transferable and transactional. Rather than guilt becoming transformative, empathy asks that it be replaced by a secondhand, first-person experience of an event that could lead to action, regardless of the authenticity of experience.

In *The Cultural Politics of Emotion*, Sara Ahmed argues that the empathetic gaze demands the passivity of the Other as a "negation that is already felt as suffering."[17] It is a passivity in which suffering becomes the passion of other people, in as much as it is a doubling down of past suffering. Through rendering the body as a vessel to be occupied by a permanent state of suffering and colonizing experience, empathy performatively enacts additional suffering. The empathetic gaze seeks suffering. Empathy is appealing because, in reinforcing the passivity of suffering people, suffering people are left behind and reduced to their circumstances and oppression.

The primary emotions of a person objectified by empathy experiences are not experienced by choice: they are a reaction. Reactions, in the power hierarchy of emotional response, are "'lower' as a sign of weakness" so that the controlled, predictable, designed, and reason-based experience by choice emotions of the empathizer remain "elevated."[18] It is imperative to not lose sight of who is rendered passive by history, society, culture, and colonization. The bodies, experiences, pasts, and whole beings of the people left behind are reduced to empty vessels for the elevated emotional state that is touted as the cure for any given social ill and called "empathy." By focusing on the experience of the Other, by going further and claiming to occupy it, the empathizer does not have to confront their culpability in reproducing social injustices, oppression, and marginalization.

Letting go of the empathetic gaze is not asking a person to be neutral. Instead, it is a demand that a person be truthful about the biases they hold and open to experience, voices, and realities of others, even if they are excluded from the experience of the Other. It is the ability to acknowledge the biases we have in our own analysis, and to understand the experience of others. It is an acknowledgment that even in our own work, we reproduce the thing we are fighting against. In this book, for instance, when I take a colonial photograph and reproduce it, I reproduce colonization even as I attempt to expand the context of the photograph. When I take in images of the Other, especially when the Other is suffering and distant, my colonial gaze will more quickly attempt to go toward empathy and feeling for and as the Other instead of feeling guilt about my inability to fix things—even if interrogation of that guilt and the other complex emotions that bubble up have the potential to be transformative and turn into meaningful actions of more productive ways of being and engaging with humanity. Empathy has the potential to stop me from questioning for whom the story needs to be told this way versus another, and who is given voice and authority. The academic gaze in the archive is just another empathy manhunt, to borrow from Ross Truscott who, in reading Chamayou, states that empathy "is a technology of hunting" that, with the human at the center as prey, "gives the hunt its 'supreme excitement,' its pleasure: one is not merely hunting an animal, but rather, an animalized human who is not like the hunter."[19]

Seeing the other side of empathy, the side where so many people find themselves, requires a radical turn. To radically engage with people and not their stories, whiteness must stop being the frame. Those on the other side must be allowed to be complicated, whole people with agency and choices instead of being limited by systems of oppression or lack of care. Rather than filtering the experience of those culturally deemed "Other" by institutions and structures of power, those "Other" people are the focus. People cannot be stand-ins for structures that limit their being. They are whole, despite the fact of whiteness and white supremacy, colonization, and modernity seeing them as incomplete. Whiteness is neither essential nor permanent. To make it so transforms white feelings into the only valid feelings. Whiteness demands that we care for white guilt rather than taking restorative and decolonial action. It moves through the world as though it is a human zoo and interprets the world through the empathetic gaze.

I am interested in the ways technology, media, archives, and culture come together to make sense of the banality of suffering at scale, often through the reliance on or imposition of empathy as the catch-all affective turn. I am fascinated by how the individual is pulled into various problematic situations or technological projects through the deployment of empathy as a rational goal, as discussed in "Mathematics Black Life" by Katherine

McKittrick: "Breathless, archival numerical evidence puts pressure on our present system of knowledge by affirming the knowable (black objecthood) and disguising the untold (black human being)."[20] If we've lost control of the archives, we must move to control our emotions. We cannot stop the bleed of meaning and humanity, but surely there is a stoppage if we make the emotional point of departure for everyone the suffering of the Other. The body moving socially as an archive of the dark past encounters the same reads through the epidermalization of the archive: "In many ways, the racial economy of the archive begins a story that demands our betrayal of the archive itself."[21]

As I think through empathy in this book, I will repeatedly return to a central idea: that empathy is itself a form of innovative media (a tool) by which the empathizer's body becomes the medium for abstracting and internalizing the experience of the Other. To state this boldly: *Empathy is a medium for suffering, and its message is the retraumatization, as imagined through the white gaze and other power structures, of the persons who are actively suffering, suffered in the past, and their descendants.* Decolonization and time are central frameworks for understanding the "other side of empathy." Letting go of empathy must be central to any decolonial project as we work across differences to imagine and create new worlds. The Other, unfeeling and unreal, as birthed and killed through empathy, is incapable of fostering a critical awareness of the self.

The Other, as experienced through empathy, is defined by a tragic past through which everything is filtered. Empathy disregards actual interactions with the Other and disables the possibility for a dialogue. The person who comes into being through empathy stops in time through the same mechanism. The more intense the suffering of a person or group is, the more likely the person or group is to being consumed and arrested. People involved in empathy on both sides are understood as mediums of experience. The closest the two sides come to having a shared experience is a form of citationality, marred by the structures of culture, where the dominant position will hold more authority than the actual experience and people on the other side.

Them.

Empathy is the embodiment of a colonial sentimentality based on missionary thinking. People with more power, put in the position to empathize, point to the people who are more oppressed, with whom they can empathize in lieu of understanding their own suffering. People with more power empathize with those who are allowed no other story. Occasionally, people with more power come up with plans to help or to speak for these wretched or damned people who have less power, so that the damned wretched may have a bit more of something (but never everything, and never equal, and never power). When helping or speaking for the damned wretched fails, the people in power point to those with less and enforce a collective understanding by those caught between the two groups: "At least we are not as bad off as them. They must really deserve it." It is important to note that the belief in a group "deserving" certain types of suffering is oriented toward the past. Some past action or circumstance of the individual or group, even if the interaction was generations prior, allows for this type of empathy and its subsequent failure when it bumps against distress.

As Fanon has argued, "The structure of the present work is grounded in temporality. Every human problem cries out to be considered on the basis of time, the ideal being that the present always serves to build the future. And this future is not that of the cosmos, but very much the future of my century, my country, and my existence."[22] The statement "these people are backwards" refers not to a spatial location of people, but rather, denotes a temporal orientation, always past, never capable of creating a future. Other words are often used to denote a similar temporality, such as "primitive," "savage," "boorish," "uncivilized," "undeveloped/developing," "unrefined," "unsophisticated," "uncultured," and so on. Empathy is an inherently colonial phenomenon as it tries to tie the ontological present to an imagined past through mind or psychic control.

Empathy cannot exist without history.[23] This control feels like embodiment, which then defines and creates the future. It does this by ensuring there is always a group denoted as primitive, uncultured, uncivilized, or boorish. In empathy, the Other is reobjectified and voiceless to ensure the Other can be either ignored, saved, or condemned not by themselves but by those who have the liberty of their imagination becoming reality. I understand decolonization to be a project of undoing. Letting go of empathy and facing its other side is a decolonial project. Understanding decolonization as an orientation toward the future complicates empathy, as empathy creates a false engagement with the past. Empathy erases the present and denies those who are not part of the existing power structures, those who are only real through empathy, the ability to be part of the future. This is an enforced affective incompleteness for those who exist outside of the dominant power structures.

I do not have an answer to how we might replace empathy other than that an affect suitable to the task of decolonization must start with radical love of the self and the Other. What I do have are thoughts on the temporality bound in colonial ideals of goodness and badness, of missions, and almost humans, where we might imagine what might become if we replace empathy with mutual recognition, action, and perhaps compassion. Without compassion based on a radical transcendent self-love, to let go of empathy does not stop the self-alienation and annihilation so central to colonial thinking and designed to launch people into a psycho-existential crisis that requires the Other so the self can be defined and valued.

Us.

In *The Colonization of Psychic Space* Kelly Oliver suggests "the negative affects of the oppressors are 'deposited into the bones' of the oppressed. Affects move between bodies; colonization and oppression operate by depositing the unwanted affects of the dominant group onto those othered by that group in order to sustain its privileged position."[24] The unwanted suffering and pain of oppression are the domain of empathy. Empathy forces these dynamics into a cyclical configuration by displacing temporalities and asking people to step into a painful past when that past is not their own. In empathy culture, we look toward the past and see empathy even when empathy did not yet exist.

Often, when I speak with people about empathy, they ask why I do not cite Saidiya Hartman's *Scenes of Subjection* more. Hartman's first chapter does a deep dive into the slipperiness of empathy, which will be engaged in later chapters. Though the book's discussion is useful, the example in the book is a predecessor to empathy and not quite empathy. For me, this illustrates the "us" problem. The colonization of empathy and empathy culture is so universal, we have lost the ability to speak of things or understand things in other ways, or even to imagine anything before empathy. This allows modern society to believe that today's choices are based on a better and more ethical understanding of the Other because empathy is at our cultural core. What this elides is that certain bodies are allowed to exist only as an empathetic death. The structures of society contain and limit their potential while the imagined endless suffering infects the present as an infestation of the empathetic gaze. The desire to frame things through empathy causes an engagement with the past based on confirmation biases.

And then there is me.

Letting go of the empathetic gaze is not asking a person to be neutral. Instead, it is a demand to be truthful about the biases we harbor and open to the experiences, voices, and realities of Others. It is an acknowledgment that I am excluded from the experience of the Other. It is the ability to acknowledge the biases I have in my own analysis and understanding of the experience of Others. It is acknowledging the reproduction of colonial and other problematic dynamics inherent in doing my own work, even as I fight against those dynamics.

In chapter 1, "The other side of human zoos," I attempt to unflatten the shame, guilt, and anger that we inherit, which causes us both to confront people with their own oppression in an effort to understand them and to form affective responses through empathy that limit the narratives we tell. In this chapter, I look at two contemporary critical and historical studies of nineteenth-century exhibitions in the United States and Europe of colonized people and others put on display for the amusement and edification—and, of course, sentiments—of visitors. I am as interested in the role empathy plays as a critical apparatus for twenty-first-century scholars looking back to the nineteenth century as well as its role in the nineteenth-century gaze these scholars reconstruct. Photographs of exhibits and, indeed, nineteenth-century photographs are also key to the "human zoo" of twenty-first-century publications. I am affected by photographs as I search through digital archives and the winding paths they create to learn more about people whose photographs have the potential to spread digitally and decontextualized.

In chapter 2, "We have names," I look at human zoos and their related remnants through the medium of photography. I recontextualize colonial photographs of a girl named Héiliani from Oubangui Chari, French Congo, who became the cover model of a coffee table photography book called *Eve Noire* years before this random photograph was digitized with additional biographic information. I also expand the narrative of a series of photographs from 1888 of "Hottentots,"[25] members from various tribes in South Africa, that included men, women, and children, brought to Paris, France, to be examined by scientists and then put on exhibition at the Jardin d'Acclimatation. With both these groups of photographs, I explore beyond their archives to piece together who people may have been rather than getting caught up in my feelings about their suffering, which has already been reproduced countless times across culture and research. I explore how images are often used to highlight the subject's suffering without questioning the structures that created this suffering or allowing the subjects to be more. Historical photography is an important medium to explore because it paved the way for the culturally mediated empathy culture of today by showing far away "colonies" and their people to Western audiences mediated by a lens rather than by the words (as in novels or stories) or the hands (as in drawings and paintings) of another.

Finally, in chapter 3, "New media and emerging technology will kill us all, though," I think through the limits of the current technological trends with emerging media and the new ways we encounter other people through the literal and metaphoric lens of technology often marketed as "enhancing empathy." I explore virtual reality, touted as "the empathy machine," and the VR project "Becoming Homeless," which highlights some of the limits of focusing on the first-person perspective. I also explore the MIT project, "Deep Empathy AI," which attempts to crowdsource an empathetic response, and other experiments in AI. Finally, I engage the concept of the digital twin to highlight how, with technology, even the self becomes Other through data that is more real and valid, which is the ultimate end of colonization. I look at the rise of empathy as a central cure-all and tie this to the themes of race, colonial exploitation, and dehumanizing empathy.

What the world today highlights, with digital movements and their inherent disjointedness, is something that has always been true. Understanding and knowledge-production will always create something incomplete for the people and objects of study. Reconstruction is an impossibility. In deciding to create something, I am sharing my knowledge and perspective as though it is whole and complete. The format of its delivery will validate this. I am not the whole, though, and my people and objects of study will never be, either. I am writing into the incomplete. This book is an attempt to bring sense to the disjointed, messy, coherent, and incoherent that come from doing digitally born or digitally augmented work. It is about sitting with the sources, feelings, and ideas that fill in spaces, seeing connection, and looking for more.

This book is an attempt to do trauma-informed work while minimizing the need to retraumatize in order for the story to be more complete. Through algorithms and scripted experiences that purport to be elevated forms of feeling, the digital world seeks to create empathy machines to reframe suffering and oppression. These technologies attempt to dictate how and what our affective responses should be in ways powerfully analogous to the "human zoos" of the nineteenth century, which is why it is important to reexamine what we know about human zoos. I argue that we do not need to accept this future. We have the ability to do more. This book is an attempt to rethink the technologies of empathy in order to decolonize a popular affect and, beyond that, to find other, complex emotions that are more meaningful and truly transformative. In writing *The Other Side of Empathy,* I hope to open a space for people to have feelings about their own formative encounters that shape the world and the past to help us move toward a more equitable and complete future.

1: The other side of human zoos?

The past is but the mirror of the future.
—Eugène Huzar, *La fin du monde par la science*

There are two books. One is *Human Zoos: The Invention of the Savage* and the other is *From Samoa with Love?*[1] Both books are companions to museum shows, but they take very different approaches to re-aestheticizing and revisiting the past of people put on display at ethnographic shows in zoos and gardens and at various events across Europe.

The introduction to *Human Zoos: The Invention of the Savage*, written by the president of the Musée du Quai Branly, contains the following text:

> From sordid to commercial, reaching the heights of indecency, human zoos, circuses, fairs, ethnic exhibits, freak shows and other spectacles staged the exploitation and dispossession of certain humans by other humans. They opened the door to realms of imagination that this exhibition masterfully reconstructs.[2]

This framing regurgitates and reignites the colonial gaze and its oppression but the authors (and the exhibit's curators) imagine the show and book as doing the opposite: "By giving them a name, a life and a history, we free these people from the shackles in which they were once held, restoring dignity to individuals who suddenly found themselves thrust on stage in front of a curious crowd simply because they were considered different."[3]

The attempt at showing a broader humanity has already failed. Simple pleasure is derived from flipping through the book's pages, which are covered in illustrations and photographs used to advertise human zoological exhibitions. Each page is a spectacle. The text reads more like a textbook than a critical or restorative engagement.

Focusing on the impact of a German man by the name of Carl Hagenbeck and the financial impetus for putting people on display suggests that these are the important aspects of this history. Little is done to expand on the lives of the people framed in the images on these pages. Instead, the book serves as a re-exhibition tool. A death occurs in telling the stories of the zoos rather than showing the lives of these people and how they came to be in these exhibitions. If the goal of the new exhibit was to do more, its curators failed. The title, framing, and fetishization of visuals recontextualized by the book reinvents the "savage" and the "freak." The book serves as a confirmation of how and who we should look at as an enduring curiosity. The book and exhibit, as described, mimic the physical show, with the goal of allowing patrons to relive a deeply problematic past, despite its inhumanity, without having to actually face people. This allows visitors to explore the "realms of imagination that this exhibition masterfully reconstructs." The design enables pleasure in oppression. Just as before, the effect is people making money from the exploitation of Others, from Carl Hagenbeck to the director of the museum today.

From Samoa with Love? takes a different approach, despite being on a similar subject and from the same type of organization. The exhibit this book analyzes took place at the Museum Fünf Kontinente in Munich, Germany, in 2014. Rather than starting with the president of the museum, it starts with an acknowledgment from a descendant of the Samoans who were exhibited in Germany, His Highness Tui Ātua Tupua Tamasese Efi. This small but radical act displaces the primacy of the museum by acknowledging the voices who were missing and giving them space and agency in a way that was not afforded to them in the past. The book humanizes and expands their histories through photographs. The preface takes a radical turn by acknowledging that history can, and should, be shattered by the places that fabricated the mirrors of oppression and exploitation in which society is asked to see itself today:

> Careful and meticulous research of the collections kept in our museum is part of our basic mission as a museum of ethnology. In light of global discourses on the history of ethnological museums, their historical

responsibility and present-day significance it is critical to pay due attention to the contextualization of objects.[4]

The book's deeply researched essays contextualize archives, oral histories, travel documents, and memorabilia. The ending of the book was used to "hear" from a contemporary artist of Samoan, Tahitian, and Cook Island descent, Michel Tuffery. His work grapples with the legacy of this history. The series was shown alongside historical objects and photographs. His work includes paintings depicting modified historical photographs, intricately carved wooden combs inspired by combs seen in portrait photographs, and film of an open-air media experience on the topic in Samoa. This art, on display with the historical objects, creates a link to the past.

Tuffery's artwork highlights today's possibility for understanding the past when the experience of someone who inherited its legacy is foregrounded. The beauty of using the word *talofa* is that it keeps the focus on the people who were on display not as spectacle but as people with cultures, history, and agency.[5] The exploitation is examined in a way that prevents evacuating the people of their humanity and making them into signifiers of oppression and exploitation. The photos in the book are handled with care, positioned as beautiful portraits of people who lived through this experience and had reasons for doing so. Every aspect of the book is designed to make readers challenge their assumptions and acknowledge more than historical oppression.

The title, *From Samoa with Love?* forces the viewer or reader to question what is actually being seen with love. Rather than continuing to force a European sentimentality on the past and the people, the title calls attention to the way objects, words, and people were brought together, and it forces the acknowledgment of German complicity in the continued exploitation and disenfranchisement of Samoa and American Samoa. The reader of the book is pushed inside the story, too. The tug-of-war between oppression, beauty, complexity, and agency forces a reframing of where to place importance and how to connect not through empathy around the imagined experience but through *talofa*. The museum went about meticulously reconstructing the journey and experience from Samoa to Germany and matching people with the stories and photographs. They then took the stories and photographs to descendants: "For a number of descendants those were particularly emotional moments, since they had known their ancestors, if at all, only as elderly people and had been unaware of the existence of photographs showing them as young men and women."[6] The German people who came to the show would come back with boxes of photographs from family members who had been in colonial Samoa. By acknowledging their complicity in concealing the bigger narrative of German Samoa, they were freed from what Allan Sekula calls the shadow archive.[7]

Today.

The heritage of human zoos is often relegated to the past. People in the past were operating under a moral, legal, and ethical code different from today. They did not have the ability to make different choices. Empathy slips so easily from caring for the person on display to those in power. It is more comfortable there. Putting people on display as a form of divertissement at the cost of a ticket is a thing of the past. But things are still the same. The dynamics of technologically mediated empathy culture and the sentimentality it generates cannot be understood without understanding the dynamics of human zoos.

$$Now + Us > Them (\infty Past)$$

The first time I went to Hawai'i, I was in high school. We were tourists staying in Waikīkī and running around Honolulu doing normal tourist things. At the time I was in a photography class. I brought my camera and my self-wound black-and-white film rolls. I was on the hunt, loaded and ready to shoot my final project, a photo-essay. I was assured the highlight of this trip was going to the Polynesian Cultural Center. We boarded a bus in Waikīkī and arrived in Lā'ie an hour later. Lā'ie is a former sugarcane plantation settled in the late 1800s by missionaries of the Church of Latter-day Saints (the Mormon Church). By the mid 1900s, the focus of the settled land shifted:

> The Polynesian Cultural Center, situated on the north-eastern coast of Oahu, the main island of Hawai'i, offers a spectacular example of the theatricalization of Polynesian culture. Founded in 1963 under the aegis of the Mormon church, this "cultural theme park" (the PCC's self-description) houses seven Polynesian villages. The Polynesian cultures represented (Hawai'i, Tahiti, Marquesas, Samoa, Tonga, New Zealand (Māori), and Fiji) are staged in various ways for the tourist gaze. The "actors" are students of the adjacent Brigham Young University (Hawai'i campus), who assume various theatrical tasks as they perform their own cultures in a putatively "traditional" form.[8]

A trip to the many island nations of Polynesia is not logistically possible in a single day. The archipelagos are fairly isolated. Some are independent

POLYNESIAN VILLAGE TOURS

Travel through time and space as you experience thousands of years worth of culture from six different island nations, each with its own flavor and appeal.

OPEN 3:45–5:00PM (UNTIL APRIL 24)

TONGA TAHITI

PACIFIC THEATER

HUKILAU MARKETPLACE

PRIME DINING

POUNDERS RESTAURANT

ALI'I LUAU

FIJI HAWAII

AOTEAROA

SAMOA

Fig 1.1. Map of the Polynesian villages. Courtesy of the Polynesian Cultural Center, https://polynesia.com/villages/.

or part of different countries. Disconnected from time and space, as the website says, visitors "travel through" the islands all at once. There is even a map (figure 1.1) that brings them together, creating imaginary proximity and sameness.

Thousands of years of history and space across the ocean are compressed into a single immersive experience. If there are questions visitors might not feel comfortable asking the "natives," there are missionary houses with live white missionaries able to answer any question a visitor might have. It is impossible to imagine the Polynesian students' day-to-day clothing. The students are outside of time. Their job is not to show their lives today but rather the past of their ancestors. The Polynesian Cultural Center presents stand-ins who, by virtue of being descendants of people previously shown, are capable of tapping into some essential imagined form and feeling of Polynesia. Even in the good there is an underlying objectification. If something "travels through time and space," then it is already removed from belonging anywhere. The people are "an experience," not an act or event.

I remember Samoa at the Polynesian Cultural Center. There was a man covered in tattoos wearing nothing but a lavalava, the brightly colored skirt-like garment worn by men. He yelled "*Talofa!*" and, with a huge smile, started talking about his daily life in Samoa with a bit too much enthusiasm. "I am a chief," he said. And he was going to show us how they gathered food and leaves to cook with from the trees every morning. Just as the Samoans in Germany had done almost one hundred years before, he climbed a forty-foot coconut tree. He seemed to go out of his way to make it feel unthreatening to the audience through his use of self-deprecating comments. It unsettled my stomach. I later recognized this feeling as described in Fanon's "Y a bon Banania" discussion in *Black Skin, White Masks*.[9] I, a brown skinned woman who in Hawai'i was assumed to be Polynesian, watched the audience instead of him. We were surrounded by a gaggle of white people in awe of the spectacle. I saw something I still cannot put into words. I disengaged. We stayed at the Polynesian Cultural Center for most of the day, hopping from island performance to island performance. But by the time the big show at the end started, I asked if we could go back to the hotel. My photo-essay had no story. It was just a series of photographs of flowers at the Polynesian Cultural Center, because I couldn't bring myself to gaze at the performers long enough to shoot.

Given the Mormon Church's stance on modesty and body modification, the traditional clothing and tattoos of the performers highlighted the slippage of time at the cultural center. The Mormon students as performers were playing people who do not know they are immodest. The president of the Polynesian Cultural Center, P. Alfred Grace, spoke on this in the LDS *Living* article "Why There Are Tattoos and Strapless Costumes at the Polynesian Cultural Center" (Sandau, 2019). According to Grace, the center wants to honor the parts of culture in line with doctrine. The center also does its best to be respectful of the communities and cultures of the student-performers. As such, if students are Samoan and have the neck-down traditional tattoos before they come to BYU and the Polynesian Cultural Center, they can show them because the tattoos are still important in Samoan culture. However, they should not go home and get tattoos and come back with them. Women's clothing is modified to not show their midriffs. They are not allowed to drink kava, a ceremonial drink, which played a pivotal role in the German Samoan shows described in *From Samoa with Love?*, because it is abused. But it is fine to drink kava when they go home.[10]

Customers who visit the Polynesian Cultural Center pay to see Polynesia as they imagine it to be. With the exception of the Hawaiian students, the students at the Polynesian Cultural Center are far from their sacred lands. The students have a reason for performing at the center: they are supporting themselves. Since 1963, the church's stance is they are saving cultures on the brink of being lost forever without acknowledging that missionaries were one of the biggest contributors to cultural loss. Missionaries forbade people from speaking in their mother tongues and made them ashamed of their own sacred stories and rituals:

> The project was the Polynesian Cultural Center which was to be constructed on college land adjacent to the campus. Wendell B. Mendenhall said that cultures of the Polynesian peoples are "on the brink of oblivion." Therefore the chief purpose of the village is to keep the Polynesian cultures alive for posterity.
>
> Prior to this time, a Polynesian Institute had been established at the Church College. The goals stated for the institute at its inception were:
>
> 1. To assist the Pacific Island peoples in making the social, psychological, economic, and political adjustments to the circumstances of modern life;
> 2. To give the people of the Pacific a pride in their cultural heritage;
> 3. To present to the public at large an insight into the beauty and dignity of traditional Polynesian life;
> 4. To preserve through films, recordings, written descriptions, and explanations and through transference from generation to generation the entertainment culture of Polynesia;
> 5. To preserve through training the arts and crafts whereby the Polynesian met the physical needs and aesthetic urges of his simple life;
> 6. To provide means of support for the South Pacific students at the Church College of Hawaii through scholarships and work opportunities in the Polynesian Cultural Center;
> 7. To provide outlets for manufactured items from Latter-day Saints in the South Pacific;
> 8. To be an agency within the Pacific School System through which information about educational and social programs can be disseminated to administrators and teachers within that system;
> 9. To acquaint people everywhere with the work of the Church of Jesus Christ of Latter-day Saints.[11]

What you'll experience.

If you like to laugh—a lot—come see one of the Center's most popular cultural presentations where you will learn how to crack open a coconut using a small rock, marvel as our strong young men climb 40-foot coconut trees in their bare feet and see what happens when you combine fire and sharp weapons. Speaking of fire, can you start one with two sticks? In Samoa, yes you can! You can also learn how to twirl a fire knife, weave a basket, and cook bananas. As you stroll through our village, take a moment to notice how the unusual domed shaped buildings are constructed without nails and how they create their own natural air conditioning.[12]

The Samoan Polynesian Cultural Center performance is the same performance that Samoans gave in Germany at various zoos and fairs between 1900 and 1901.[13] The feature section for Samoa on the "Island Villages" page (figure 1.2) looks like a promotional poster from the past. There is a man high up in a tree, and a play button so you can click on the video. Below, there is a man smiling, dressed in traditional clothing and seated next to a fire where another man is doing some unclear traditional task. In another, people are sitting around eating, and one person is holding a kava bowl (given that it is forbidden, who knows what's in it). In the last image, a father and son sit next to man blowing on a big smokey bowl. The text on the promo page reads, "Feel the heat, show some muscle, enjoy the Samoan song and dance and marvel as a young warrior climbs a 40-foot coconut tree-in his bare feet. Become a part of the 'happy people' at the Samoan Village."

Though the term "noble savage" or "heathen" are never there, the juxtaposition of warrior with "happy village" and the images do the work of conveying those terms. Having people on display becomes the object of colonial pleasure, a space where empathy is not possible because "y'a bon Banania": *This is for their own good. Without us here to see their primitive ways and bring them to Light, they are damned.*[14] And so we come to the other side of empathy, the side where the oppressed and exploited are demonized for still being joyful. Questions are repeated as people from outside the communities facing oppression have encounters or work with people from these cultures. A life fully consumed by the performance of the savage diverts people from the reality of oppression and revels in the pleasure of it. Viewers mistake the performance for authenticity. Recognition of primitive people becomes a moment of jouissance, a party atmosphere

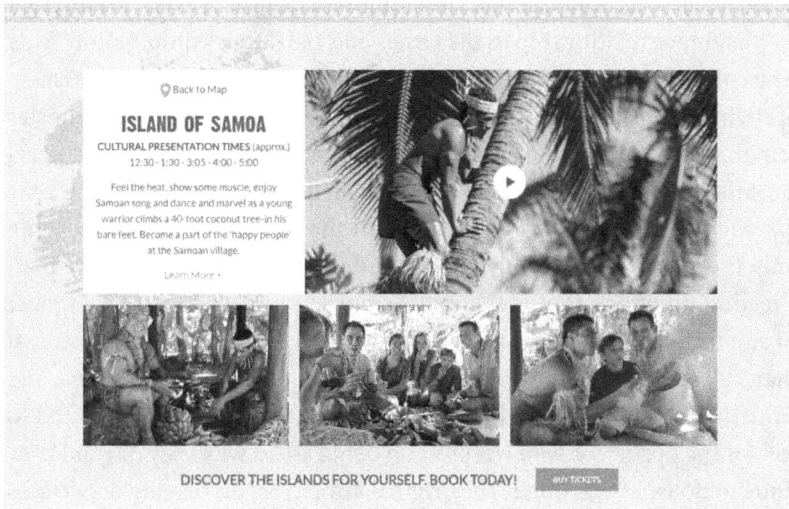

Fig 1.2. Introduction to the Island Samoa. Courtesy of the Polynesian Cultural Center, https://polynesia.com/villages/.

with lights and music to ensure that it is felt the right way. A stated goal of the Polynesian Cultural Center is "to present to the public at large an insight into the beauty and dignity of traditional Polynesian life," which comes directly from the stated goals of the Polynesian Cultural Center listed previously.

I am guilty of seeing the Polynesian Cultural Center only as a continuation of colonial oppression and feeling for the student-performers who did not realize what was being done to them. What dignity comes with such a harsh judgment and so much colonial baggage? People in power and the structural forms of oppression are obscured by the person on display to the point that the performer is no longer recognized as fully human. This is where empathy is born. My judgment is baseless, but it became the whole picture for me. I missed the show and learned nothing. I am dehumanized by mistaking the oppressive structures and historical baggage for the people who are simply living their lives.

The body carries the story of suffering and imagined suffering. The horrors of the past can be judged by today's moral standards. We must judge. We must judge because the horrors of the past are today's moral standard. The horrors of the past determine the dominant gazes of today: white supremacy, colonization, oppression, and marginalization. The past is carried forward and inscribed in the minds and eyes of everyone through an imaginary relationship to the Other and the Other's domination. Men who commit monstrous acts are memorialized through the nameless faces of their victims and by people who resemble their victims. The monster remains a faceless white space, because it is morally acceptable to create suffering but not to be held accountable for its creation. And with the distance of time, the words to speak of the atrocities are lost, leaving only the binary of suffering and not suffering, which is little more than a feeling. In effect, to understand the burden of suffering is to connect to suffering as though it were one's own, and my suffering is more real than the suffering of the Other. The suffering of the Other is undone, and empathy is called forward because the oppressed are always expected to feel for the oppressor who weeps upon being asked why they did and continue to do what was done. The original atrocity is lost leaving only traces behind in culture.

Mediation obscures our ability to meaningfully engage difference by flattening space, time, and culture, sometimes under the guise of globalization. Globalization is a stand-in for war. Harold Innis argues that to feel as the Other centers the self: "In using other cultures as mirrors in which we may see our own culture we are affected by the astigmatism of our own eyesight and the defects of the mirror, with the result that we are apt to see nothing in other cultures but the virtues of our own."[15] To imagine the Other as expansive or universal limits the understanding of culture to those things that remind a person of their own. Structures of oppression and inequality continue to exist. The retreat to empathy adds abstraction and interiorization to the structures, placing blame and culpability on individuals instead of on systems. Historically, technologies, namely the press, photographs, and transportation improvements allowed people to become objects for exhibitions, zoos, and traveling ethnological shows. As electronic means of visual mediation advanced to include film and television (and today digital technology), these types of encounters waned. The gaze shifts toward certain people on the other side of empathy. If the content of emerging technologies and new media is always already the production of the Other under the auspices of colonization, imperialism, and globalization, then decolonization must "other" technology and its cultural role. This is done through the drive to archive, remediate, sort, and catalog. Modern technology seems to come from nostalgically looking toward the near past. The nostalgic hopes of technology creators are pushed forward as the future.

Of beastly men and the damned archive.

us ≠ ∞Past

The system of violent domination that societies collectively live under today, in which some men lord above all others, was born in Europe and perfected in the transatlantic slave trade. Today, that system continues in global corporations, new colonization, and the disenfranchisement of dominated people. This is war. Countless named white men who perpetrate the war for white ideological dominance continue to own the past and, thus, the future. Ancestors of the dominated are left to languish in their inability to escape the narrative of the world these men created. As for the white descendants of those white men, the gleeful propensity toward violent destruction of any-one and anything standing in their way remains. When dominated people's suffering is palatable and the smells of fear and pain fill their nostrils, when the energy in the air is that of despair, people relish in it. Empathy lets them know they've done a good job. The named white men christen this "power." However, as Prophecy Coles argues, the turn to empathy risks great losses: "We must not ignore ... the impact of our ancestral history, especially if our ancestors have suffered, for their anguish can return and haunt us. It is the anguished return of traumatic experience that repeats itself across generations and affects the way the next generation is perceived."[16] Trauma returns and the crisis haunts. Empathy renders the past ghostly.

Likewise, bias is carried by empathy, rendering racism a literacy for understanding: "In attempting to understand the origins of racism, it is important to avoid removing it to a historical past or displacing its sources onto the oppressed. Any investigation or representations of [Otherness], then, must take a critical look at Euro-American whiteness to understand the construction of race as a category"; as critic Brian Wallis has insisted, "To ignore white ethnicity is to reduce its hegemony by naturalizing it."[17] Power creates knowledge. Knowledge becomes history. Historical memory and the places that collect, curate, and keep the past are hellbent on making the same grave choices (violent mistakes and omissions) of the named white men: this preserves the current social order. Designated and recognized spaces hold hegemonic whiteness, ensuring colonial ideologies remain universal across societies. Nothing as subjective and porous as empathy will break down structures and institutions, because empathy reifies and is mediated through networks of proximity and contains the biases and violence of power.

In "From Human Rights to Feminist Ethics: Radical Empathy and the Archives," Michelle Caswell and Marika Cifor argue that "empathy is radical if it is directed precisely at those we feel are least worthy, least deserving of it."[18] If, as a coworker told me, the "archives authenticate content as being true or historically valid," and if knowledge is a site of colonial struggle as Walter Mignolo and Catherine Walsh state, we must then allow ancestral history to come forth from voices silenced, interrupted, co-opted, and erased in the archive. Empathy must not give a person or institution dominion over the voices of Others. Likewise, one must not demand that Others have specific kinds of empathy entwined in whatever judgment is contained in "least worthy." Radical empathy in this configuration is wholly colonial. I reserve my right to say screw Carl Hagenbeck and any sentimental shenanigans that ask me to empathize with a man who titled his memoir *Beasts and Men*. Said memoir ends with the following:

> Here then, I must conclude my account of the many animal friendships that I have formed in the course of my life. I am continuing to develop my park on the lines already followed; and trust that, both in the exhibits of wild beasts and in those of wilde men, I shall ever succeed more completely in rendering it, not a place of captivity, but a happy and contented home. With the help of an able staff of assistants, whose experience now extends over several decades, I hope to make my institution unique in all the world as a centre for the friendly intercourse of great gathering of BEASTS AND MEN.[19]

Colonial realities connect the past with the present. Colonial realities are imagined into being to further the project of modernity through the archives and other tools of collective memorialization. These tools ensure that only certain imaginations, the ones based on the violence of colonization, become reality. If "Radical empathy is thus a learned process of human commonality through thinking and feeling into the minds of others;" and if "this bond exists even if the archivist and record creator have never met in person, even if centuries separate the record creator from the archival intervention"—because, "What archivist, after meticulously sorting through pages of diaries, folders of correspondence, and boxes of ephemera, has not felt emotionally connected to the creator of a collection?"—then the possibility for radical empathy in the archives has already realized its own failure.[20] The empathetic archive is incapable of allowing breaks from now and the past because everything has to be divined through the self of the archives today, where "self" is defined through the past's system of power. I find myself continually asking, why empathy? Of the many things for which empathy is a stand-in, the most prescient ones enable those in power to speak for the imagined suffering of Others as though the suffering is their own trauma. Neutral or beautiful encounters are distorted into suffering by people in power as they struggle to map their understanding of the world onto the bodies of Others.

Hagenbeck's legacy is special; though, perhaps incomparable is a better word. Hagenbeck's method of capturing and exhibiting people in enclosures, just as he did the animals at Tierpark Hagenbeck, conquered the world and the collective imagination across time. The miniature outdoor habitats with a moat area in front of the enclosure, as seen at modern zoos, was Hagenbeck's solution for the more humane treatment of animals. The depth of his dehumanization seems bottomless, as does the zeal with which he describes how he sees the people he brought to Germany from around the world: "As I have already mentioned, they could not be described as beautiful."[21] He goes into great detail about how he and those who worked for him captured exotic animals and took them on death marches and then put the survivors on display. He does not go into detail about the process, fate, or ethical concerns when taking people on similar journeys. He talks about his "humane" methods of keeping animals and the equality between man and beast: "Brutes, after all, are beings akin to ourselves. Their minds are formed on the same plane as our minds; the differences are differences of degree only, not of kind."[22] He includes photographs of some of the people who were part of his ethnographic shows. He fails to mention the infamous story of the two doomed Inuit families he brought to his zoo—destined to go on a tour throughout Europe—who died of smallpox before they left the first city where they were exhibited. The existing information about the families comes from the diary of Abraham Ulrikab, an Inuit who went to Germany along with his family and another couple. Abraham was literate in his native tongue and wrote down his experiences. In addition to his diary, Abraham sent letters to the missionaries of the Moravian Church, where he and his family had been baptized in Labrador, Canada.

He chose to take his family to Germany to be exhibited at the Hagenbeck Zoo and to tour Europe.[23] He was enticed to go because he would be able to quickly pay off debts to the church mission. Every member of his group died of smallpox in various countries across Europe. This story is easy to tell. Though their names are mostly forgotten, Abraham, his wife Ulrike, their two daughters, Sara and Maria, and his nephew Tobias, experience the collective expectation of such experiences. Abraham's agency is erased.

Details allowing his life to be more than this experience disappear as well. The places that perpetrated these atrocities continue to thrive, while the kin of Abraham carry forward the burden of his exploitation and death.

The people of the Moravian mission where Abraham went to church warned him not to go.[24] Abraham and his family were not "heathens." They were "good Christians," unlike the shaman couple, Terrianiak and Paingo, who would die of smallpox as well. This meant the souls of Abraham and his family were more valuable in the eyes of the missionaries. They begged Abraham not to go, because being shown in the way zoos showed people was un-Christian. But he needed money, and the work sounded easy. Plus, like many who live today, he was excited to see Europe. So he went. He, his family, and their travel companions were not inoculated against smallpox before being taken to the zoo. They died.

Carl Hagenbeck showed people for profit and with little regard for their humanity and lives. He talked of his humane approach to training animals next to the stories of the animals' suffering from dehydration, heat stroke, suicide, and illness as they were transported to lands far from their own. He does not discuss the process of catching humans in detail. I have to assume that when he spoke of capturing animals, he was speaking of the process of capturing people as well. It was done to increase profits, above all else, as the market for exotic animals was saturated:[25]

> About the middle of the seventies the supply of wild beasts began to exceed the demand, and the profits on my business somewhat decreased. Some remedy for this state of affairs had to be found, and the said remedy eventually came through the chance suggestion of a friend. In 1874 I happened to be importing some reindeer, and my friend, Heinrich Leutemann, the animal painter, remarked that it would be most picturesque if I could import a family of Lapps along with them. This seemed to me a brilliant idea, and I therefore at once gave orders that my reindeer were to be accompanied by their native masters.
>
> The Lapps, conducted by a Norwegian, arrived at Hamburg in the middle of September, and Leutemann and myself went on board to welcome the little expedition. The first glance sufficed to convince me that the experiment would prove a success. Here was a truly interesting sight. On deck three little men dressed in skins were walking about among the deer, and down below we found to our great delight a mother with a tiny infant in her arms and a dainty little maiden about four years old, standing shyly by her side. Our guests, it is true, would not have

shone in a beauty show, but they were so wholly unsophisticated and so totally unspoiled by civilisation that they seemed like beings from another world. I felt sure that the little strangers would arouse great interest in Germany.

The reindeer and the Lapps were safely disembarked, but on the way up to Neuer Pferdemarkt a rather fortunate accident occurred. The deer were, of course, unaccustomed to crowds, and two of them took fright and galloped away through the town, finally taking refuge—not inappropriately—in the Zoological Gardens. My Lappic exhibition could scarcely have had a better advertisement than was afforded by this escapade.[26]

The people Hagenbeck put on display have their own stories, as well, waiting to be uncovered and pieced back together. The imaginary is the primary space of oppression and the ultimate expression of the colonial project. Hagenbeck understood how Europe would imagine the Other. To be seen by him was to risk becoming nothing more than a body-as-object that was shown to death. I try to memorize his face and cathartically tear it into millions of pieces for all the countless lives he took to fill his pockets with their blood, sweat, tears, and being. This is colonial power. The exploitation and death. The people put on display are what enabled him to keep his image clean and his belly fed. After their journey, seeing the reindeer run free, perhaps the Sámi people thought they should run, too. But where would they go so far away from their home? And what difference would it make? They would be replaced, over and over again, just as they were replacements for an overabundance of animals.

His innovation in showing people would be copied around the world. Time, cultural shifts, and technology have muted the desire for these types of shows. What once was a day trip can now be searched for, pop up in a social media feed, or watched on demand. We grapple with their legacy without facing those responsible for normalizing uncritical engagement in these activities as divertissement. Instead, we live with echoes of suffering owned by certain nameless bodies. Hagenbeck's profound impact on how we are asked to encounter people who remind us of those he displayed for profit lives on today, digitally.

On October 15, 2012, the blog *Sociological Images* published "Human Zoos at the Turn of the 20th Century."[27] The post included three souvenir postcards from a German ethnology show. The blog post started with the following text (emphasis in original):

"***TRIGGER WARNING for racism and enslavement***"

This warning, in particular, forces the reader to apprehend the performers pictured on the postcards through the narratives of racism and enslavement, foreclosing other possibilities before the photographs are even visible. This is how implicit biases are reinscribed and reified through repetition. Non-white people's only plane of meaningful existence is within the realms of "victims of racism and enslavement." The trigger warning attempts to limit the ability for those of us touched by these histories to feel joy when seeing people who look like us in favor of selling the suffering of the Other back to whiteness. Any empathy that may come from seeing these photographs or reading this post is a construct of power born from a shared history of violence and exploitation. Certain people are allowed to be encountered historically, and everyone must feel for their struggle. For everyone else, there is racism and enslavement. Descendants of people like the ones shown on the postcard can never be fully present as individuals in the conversation when the conversation starts in such a way. This trigger warning really says, "I am so sorry for your pain and suffering. I get it. I hope you do, too." Rather than creating safety, this signals danger. Loaded and ready to shoot, again and again.

The post ends with a reference to Hagenbeck's memoirs: "In his memoirs, Carl Hagenbeck praised himself, writing, 'it was my privilege to be the first in the civilized world to present these shows of different races.'" This implies a tacit understanding that the issue is not the people Wade chose to highlight photographically but instead Hagenbeck. The blog post was written in response to a German article that chose to feature a photograph of Hagenbeck and opted to not show him. Instead, the post added a trigger warning to accompany photographs of brown people. The warning shows how our biases, even when well-intentioned, frame our affective responses to certain people imagined as suffering individuals, and how easily we slip into these biases when we try to engage with the past digitally. Hagenbeck's face *should be* associated with the ecology of oppression, exploitation, and at times, kidnapping. He, not the people he captured, brought these shows into existence. He represents racism and enslavement, not those he exploited.

Concern trolling and challenging oppression with the oppressed maintains the colonial gaze and forces an empathetic response. Always situating these stories as stories about oppression and suffering disallows those photographed to have any agency or individuality. It comes with a warning: *this is going to be a difficult pill to swallow, but don't worry, we don't have to examine ourselves and our fathers, brothers, and sons.* Using non-white people

Fig 1.3. Portrait of Carl Hagenbeck, ca. 1880–90. Photograph by Thod. Reimers, Hamburg. Courtesy Library of Congress, Prints and photographs division, LC-USZ62-126747.

as props to illustrate the imagined sufferings of Others is the inheritance of whiteness. Besides, the suffering and disenfranchisement of Others is the only method by which those named white men knew how to validate the power they killed and pillaged for. Even today, when people who look like me encounter men who look like Hagenbeck, there is an implied trigger warning passed across generations in crisis. His face (figure 1.3) is the face of a person who could aim a gun at me and shoot to kill without fear of punishment. He stands in contrast to the those we may call "allies," or "fetishists" today.[28]

There is another argument that is often made about the photography and act of hunting for the next person to be put on display. Empathy and recognition are said to exist even if the structures surrounding the creation of the photograph were inhumane. This is highlighted by an observation from Ross Truscott, who states that empathy "is promoted as an affective relation that occurred in the blind spots and shadows of the colonial state, between anthropologist and their native informants, say, or between ethnographic photographers and their subjects."[29] Bertrand Lembezat is one of the people who can fall into that reading.

Lembezat was a French colonial administrator who had a more complicated colonial gaze. He wrote numerous books on the customs of the people in the colonies he was sent to.[30] Lembezat was born in Cairo and spent his military career in Africa. The African continent was his first home; the people he saw and wrote about are the people that he grew up interacting with on a daily basis.[31] He and his brother fought with the colonial troops during World War II. Despite the love for the African continent and its countries that comes through in his work, the work is complicated by the unique historical context and the uneven power dynamics between colonial subjects and colonial administrators. All of Lembezat's writings on the colonies treat the places and people he encounters and, at times, served next to, with a reverence that erases or reduces the colonial overseers to nothing more than passive observers. Is it any wonder that a book review of *Les population paiennes du Nord-Cameroun et l'Adamaoua* said:

> Perhaps the only thing missing from the manuscript is the presence of the work being done by French missionaries. More extensive developments on the recent evolution of these populations [under missionary influence] would have been nice. Despite this, this book will be the classic textbook on this region. It is a model of sympathetic understanding and scientific objectivity.[32]

The colonization of Lembezat's father made way for the colonization that Lembezat would make his own. He was a son born in the land but not of the land, unless there is an underlying belief that the land did not come into being until colonization.

Lembezat wrote a book that is different from the rest in his oeuvres, *Eve Noire*, or *Black Eve*. The book starts with words of love and beauty followed by a collection of photographs sourced from colonial repositories. The European-trained gaze we deploy when looking at African teen girls and young women in traditional vestments is questioned. The tone is different from Hagenbeck's, as Lembezat sees something different from what Hagenbeck sees; but Lembezat's gaze is still a part of colonial domination.

His gaze still holds colonial domination carried on the backs of the photographed girls and women. The work is done not to make them equal but to make them civilized enough to mirror their station in society under the colonial gaze and structures of power. But mirrors cannot love or be loved; and if we love what we see in the mirror, we are only loving ourselves.

And today.

$$me + them \neq us$$

$$because$$

$$us \gg them$$

In the essay "The North African Syndrome," Fanon states:

> This means that there is work to be done over there, human work, that is work which is the meaning of a home. Not that of a room or a barrack building. It means over the whole territory of the French nation (the metropolis and the French Union), there are tears to be wiped away, inhuman attitudes to be fought, condescending ways of speech to be ruled out, men to be humanized.
>
> Your solution, sir?
>
> Don't push me too far. Don't force me to tell you what you ought to know, sir. If YOU do not reclaim the man who is before you, how can I assume that you reclaim the man that is in you?
>
> If YOU do not want the man who is before you, how can I believe that man that is perhaps in you?
>
> If YOU do not demand the man, if YOU do not sacrifice the man that is in you so that the man who is on this earth shall be more than a body, more than a Mohammed.[33]

Empathy, as conceived by Caswell and Cifor, places the burden of change on an individual rather than doing the hard work of trying to change structures, institutions, and collective memory in a meaningful way. The "feeling out" of a relationship defined by colonial thinking inevitably leads to misplaced trigger warnings and concern trolling, at best, as throughout society the experience of human zoos is reproduced with today's empathetic gaze. The belief that the foreign colonial administrator taking photographs and notes to send back to a mother country is capable of truly seeing colonial subjects as whole people is far-fetched. All these things reproduce power through narratives of multigenerational crises with no attention paid to counter-realities. This dynamic allowed a man and his team of people catchers to believe they could create a living archive by bringing the world into the zoo. In fact, Tierpark Hagenbeck, the one where Hagenbeck's collection of "beasts and men" existed, is still an active zoo in Germany. The zoo proudly bears his name. I must return to the idea that radical empathy in the archive is empathizing with those who least deserve it and say as eloquently as possible: Fuck Carl Hagenbeck. My radical turn is acknowledging that he deserves nothing from me.

2: We have names.

It seemed that I had suffered a sea change. I was not [my name] of [where I'm from] any more. I was now a [signaling age/stage of life] colored [gendered noun or person].
—Zora Neale Hurston, "How It Feels to Be Colored Me"

The past is digitally mediated. This is an act of creation. This is a decolonial approach to a digital and archival research project conceived as a way to move on from narratives of oppression and the empathy that they enable. This is a call to piece back together the stories and voices of people caught in colonialism's explosion. We have names!

Black women who are part of large photography projects like those of the Farm Security Administration, government, and missionary colonial photography projects, typically had their photographs taken without their personal narratives attached.[1] Colonial photographs are a means of silencing portions of the past and furthering dominant narratives. Decolonization requires finding, imagining, and engaging lost voices and incorporating or leaving space for their descendants and inheritors to complete the stories: "I am off to a flying start and I must not halt in the stretch to look behind and weep. Slavery is the price I paid for civilization, and the choice was not with me. It is a bully adventure and worthwhile that I have paid through my ancestors for it."[2] To decolonize is to give those before us their time and their lives to the best of our ability. We must reject the notion that our forebears were only victims of birth and circumstance in the systems of oppression called slavery and colonization. We must complicate the narrative by unapologetically calling out and facing those in power who created this horror as well as those who continue to perpetuate these horrors across generations. This is a call to recognize, not to feel for, those who lived through and continue to live through the legacy of their ancestor's enslavement and colonization. Going back and undoing the past is impossible. But we can create new worlds by recognizing the momentum of the past and by moving away from the narratives at its center.

Types of not-tragically colored.

us ≈ them

Photographs contain their own inaudible histories. To read into a photograph is to enter into one's own multigenerational literacy and madness. "The Analyst as 'Annilist' of Inaudible Histories" explores patients who have a madness caused by the trace of histories somewhat or completely lost.[3] This causes the past to be carried forward with "no gaze, no voice, no word," because the gaze, voice, and words are held by a person and dislodged from the past. Photographs pull people out of time without narratives or history. Photographs are a nonfuture. Like empathy, photographs depend on the viewer to feel into them, into the people shown in them, without the people having a voice from the moment they were stopped by light and mechanics. In listening closely and exploring the shadows and universes of old photographs, the things the photographs may have said bubble up in whispers. From *Black Skins, White Masks*, we read:

> The explosion will not happen today. It is too soon ... or too late.
> I do not come with timeless truths.
> My consciousness is not illuminated with ultimate radiances.
> Nevertheless, incomplete composure, I think it would be good if certain things were said.
> These things I am going to say, not shout.
> For it is a long time since shouting has gone out of my life.
> So very long. ... [4]

I look at photographs of non-white people and do not see a trigger warning. I see their beauty. When I look at photographs of Black women under colonial rule, in human zoos, facing oppression, or living as enslaved people, I see kinship. I search for features and moods and expressions similar to my own family's features and moods. I feel into things not my own. This is not empathy. This is loving. This is the inheritance from the transatlantic slave trade and its loose diaspora of people separated from their kin, roots, name, and ancestral land.

The other inheritance from the transatlantic slave trade is knowing that Black lives across the diaspora are unsettled because of whiteness. The temporality of photographs is stasis.[5] Digitized photographs transform stasis into momentum. The constantly changing environment of the screen, cushioned by large swaths of information and data, creates new forms of movement. Digital photographs feel heavy. The friction of digital photographs is different, as digital photographs only appear embedded in new digital contexts while actually being viewed in a plethora of physical and cultural contexts. Digital photographs are easily modified, cropped, and annotated. They latch onto somewhere or something and are "favorited," commented on, saved, and linked to. Digital photographs have many lives and rituals simultaneously. Digital photographs are the constant movement of light. Digital photographs are digital aftershocks and momentum.

The digital aftershocks are most evident when older photographs and other materials are reborn in the digital realm. New connections are created unintentionally through metadata and hyperlinks. Momentum. New connections, hyperconnection, and disconnection are new ways of historical seeing that come into being digitally. This allows information once hidden in the archives to bubble up and over. Transformed photographs and rediscovered histories move from the margins to the center, challenging what we think we know and feel. For certain groups, the ability to digitally engage with people and objects in the past invites the longed-for guest from the hidden past to burst into light and being. Momentum. When being is not possible, empathy fills the space between literacy and madness. In a digital encounter, the viewer has no choice but to turn toward an internal self. Digitally, everything is an object or data. Even the self. Empathy is the afterthought used to engage an unexpected or incomprehensible encounter with the digital Other.

If a prerequisite for understanding the life of a Black woman is to understand all the ways she was oppressed or suffered. She cannot come into being until the prism of oppression can be applied to her whole life. Her words are reduced to utterances and her entire being is flattened into technological utterance. Her smiles, time with her family, and her day-to-day life all become oppression, which in turn makes her the representation of oppression. Trigger warning. I cannot accept this. I refuse to make this my own gaze. Understanding Black women across the diaspora is an act of creating lethargic knowledge. More often than not, the records passed from generation to generation are incomplete. Digital archives are vast but disjointed. Finding the pieces of stories hidden in photographs, connecting them, correcting them, and putting them in a unified context is difficult. But the work must be done if we are to allow other stories to exist. Oppression is only part of the story. Oppression is the part they could not control. The affordance of the digital lies in its ability to break the binary of oppression by reimagining, engaging, and reminding the self that we are the other side of yesterday, and our feelings toward the past are nostalgia. When nostalgia is understood in this manner, it is positioned as hope for the near future.

We think of ourselves in the first person through the first-person pronouns, "I," "me," and "my." We can speak to and of our personal embodied experiences. The movement through space causes a third-person existence to be placed upon the bodies of others. In the social realm, the body as matter takes up space and has a narrative constructed by the perceiving eye/I. The perception of the body as "her/him/them" is determined by the histories the body invokes and the feelings conjured in other people. To face the body as a person is to face (or put a face on) all the things on the surface of history and our current social structure.

For a Black woman, the body scripts a story we do not want to confront or write ourselves into in the first person. She is seen by many as not an "her," but an "it." Her body is heavy (mentally). Her body is big (historically). Her body engulfs (now). Her body seems to suck up the air. The actual presence of the body makes people more aware of what they say and how they say it. Scared of their own utterances, people self-censor and self-asphyxiate. Her body halts conversations and instigates others. The just, representationally present body is safe to be consumed, to speak of, and about. We are told to script and bind these bodies to a narrative of trauma. Those who recognize themselves in the images are socially made to exist in the imagined crisis of the past, because empathy requires that certain people perpetually suffer.

Digital connections create new conditions. Just as technologies bring forth their own accidents, the impossibility of self-recognition when looking toward the past (through representational media forms such as photographs) brings forth new possibilities. A viewer never has the possibility of existing within the past of photographs because photographs represent an arrested time propelled into the future. The ability to reach back into the archive to the moment of a digital object, find lost connections, and create reshaped and expanded narratives is a form of communion. This communion requires letting go of prescriptive empathy and being open to the complexities and layers of meaning inherent to a human condition such as suffering. Per Fanon, "This rediscovery, this absolute valorization almost in defiance of reality, objectively indefensible, assumes an incomparable and subjective importance."[6] Yes, there is suffering, but suffering is not what I am looking for. I am trying to find bits of life, joy, agency, and being. I search for voices and resistance against the dominant narrative. I try to find other places of connection. Afterall, empathy is a shortcut for "connection."

Héliani/Hellani.

Just as there is "a Mohamed," there is "a Black Eve:"

> This withdrawal is still more marked in some sedentary persons who see here only "savages," capable doubtless of arousing some fleeting interest, curiosity, vague eroticism if women's bodies are involved, nothing else. A shower of critical observations will support their feeling: those round, shaved heads, those androgynous masks, those angular shoulders, those spindly legs . . . and those horrible discs, that tattooing. . . . [7]

This photo is different. This is a girl "spotted" at a party who became (*devint*) the cover model for a book of photographs titled *Eve Noire*. The photographs were compiled by Bertrand Lembezat from the colonial archives (figure 2.1). The book contains a short introduction (in the French version) and a conclusion (in the English version of the same text). I am stuck on these women becoming. Seeing these women as part of a broader and more universal constellation shifts the monolithic narratives they exist within but are excluded from. I feel and continue to feel sadness, because women who look like me, women who were photographed for various reasons that were often highly problematic, are not able to exist outside of the narrative those projects created. Their reduction spreads and applies to anyone who reminds the world of their original transgression: existing. The following text is from the concluding English text of Lembezat's book:

> These women are beautiful, nevertheless, erect in the burning light of the African noonday sun, which carves in relief their muscular bodies, shining with oil for some festival, dripping as they step out of a bath, with the water glistening on their skin, fresh and black as that of a fruit; or in the softer light of the evening, going to the fountain, arched under the amphora with its serene contours, milling the grain, or, in their gestures of self-adornment, imitating eternal Eve.[8]

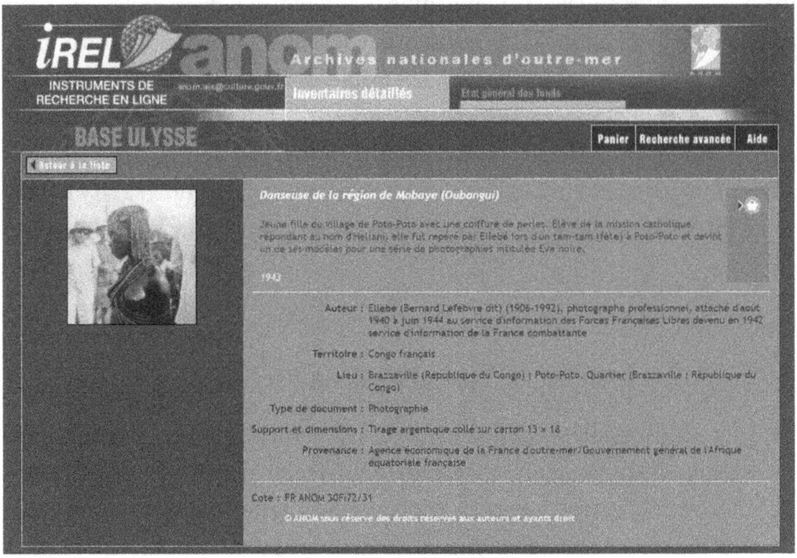

Fig 2.1 and 2.2. Two screen captures from Archive national d'outre-mer website, one featuring details about a photograph of Héliani, and the other of the page featuring the photograph. http://anom.archivesnationales.culture.gouv.fr/ulysse/notice?id=FR_ANOM_30Fi72-31.

The photo in the digital archive of Héliani dancing while being watched by white men in is not found in *Eve Noire* (figure 2.2). The gaze of the viewer is inevitably drawn to the men. As viewers we attempt to pull them into focus or imagine clearer faces of those familiar to us become the boogeymen. The colonial context consumes Héliani and gushes from the photograph like lava, burning everything in its path before turning into rocks. We recognize the gaze of the men. The blurry faces of white men erase the blurry faces of villagers who were also watching Héliani's performance. This fraction of a second in Héliani's life is the collective image society imagines but rarely sees. Héliani is the cover model (figure 2.3). She stands in an identical pose as the digital archival photograph, but from a different angle. Rather than the person holding the camera being to her side they are in front of her, probably kneeling. She looks down directly at them, into the lens, and now at anyone holding the book. This photograph says, "I am here. And I see you. I see *you*." Another excerpt from Lembezat's conclusion:

> Eve before the temptation, unaware of her nudity, carefree, laughing, avoiding shamelessness because ignorant of shame, or rather, of prudishness, ever "whose eyes astounds by its candor," and whose naive peacefulness, forever forbidden to our hearts, we readily might envy.
>   Black Eve, but what does that matter; just remember....

"I am black, but I am lovely
O Daughters of Jerusalem...."[9]

When I first found the digital photograph of Héliani, I had two nagging questions: "Is/was sharing this photograph the right thing to do?" and "Why?" I showed the photograph during a presentation and asked for initial reactions. I explained how I came across the photograph and the bit of information provided online: Héliani, a Catholic schoolgirl. A white woman listened and then, exasperated, said, "She can't be Catholic! She's naked!" as though Catholic schoolgirls are incapable of nudity. As John Berger says, "She is not naked as she is. She is naked as the spectator sees her," as are all the other "Black Eves" before and after her.[10]

Héliani remains a young girl from the village of Poto-Poto, outside of Brazzaville in the French Congo, with a hairstyle of pearls. She is a student at the Catholic mission, and she responds to the name of Héliani, the personification of Black Eve. Héliani, who with a slight glance down is captured in a photograph, represents the horrors of colonization and

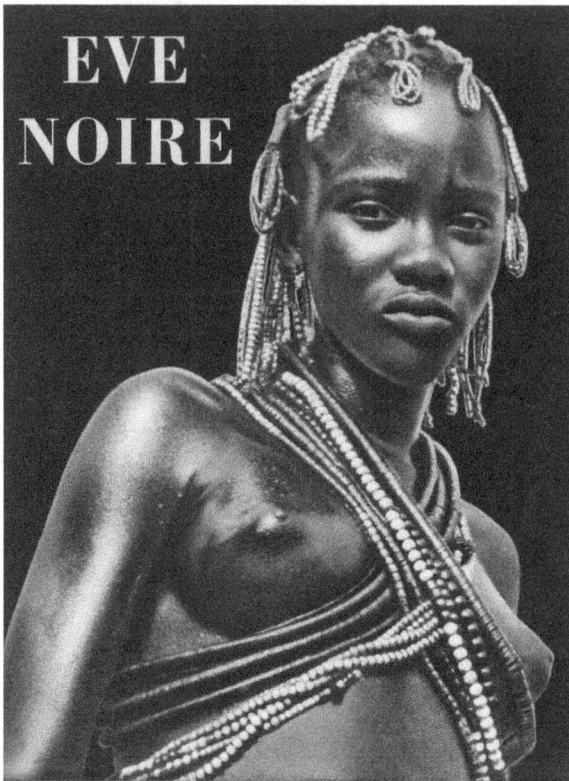

Fig 2.3. Cover of the book *Eve Noire* (Neuchatel: Editions Ides et calande, 1952) featuring Héliani. Though it is known that she was photographed by Bernard Lefebvre, the photographs in the book do not contain the names of photographers for individual photographs and instead list photographers on the title page as Bertrand Lembezat, Robert Carmet, and The Minister of Outer Seas France.

the strength to exist despite them. To decolonize the digital photograph requires negotiating the aesthetic resonances of photographs through an expanded understanding of the social conditions of its creation, and it requires remembering everything that is absent in a photograph. Her voice. The vibrant colors of dirt rubbed on her skin after she is oiled. The smell of her body glistening under the sun with sweat and movement. The kind of ecstasy of being in that moment, when the noise of the beads on her body, hands-on drums, and feet pounding against hardened earth collide: "One of the most ancient, and the most beautiful, love poems of humanity, was it not inspired by a dusky beauty?"[11]

There are more photographs of Héliani, and there is more context. Héliani's photographer, another named white man, Bernard Lefebvre (known as Ellebé), wrote a photographic memoir titled *Avec de Gaulle en Afrique*. The layout of the book (figures 2.4–2.6) allows the pictures to be read in the context of the photographer's work in addition to the lives of his subjects, from his perspective and memories. The photographs of Héliani pull you in. The length of the text is short enough that one wants to read what he has to say. He had a day of leave from his duties as military photographer and decided to travel with his "boy" translator to Poto-Poto. Upon crossing a bridge, he happened upon two sisters dancing in the river. One of them was Héliani, or Hellani as he spells her name.[12] He was struck by her beauty and statuesque body; he also calls her body aesthetically seductive. He approached her and her sister. The two girls were hesitant when he approached, but he was intrigued. He asked to follow Héliani to take photographs of her.

He respected the customs of her village and made sure that elders were always present. She was never alone. The day she modeled for him, he asked her to play in the tall grass by the river so he could take artistic shots, like the ones passed around in Paris. In the river photos, she fails to seductively splash water on herself. Instead, she smacks the water with her hands to create two splashes. She looks down on them intensely examining their quality. It looks like she is avoiding getting water on her face. She is playful. In the other, she sits, holding a leg to her chest. Her face says she is bored or annoyed. She does not look at the camera. She never executes the sensuality he was searching for. In the tall grass, she is topless and wears only a cloth around her waist. One hand grabs a bit of tall grass above her shoulder. Her other arm has a bracelet and bends at the elbow, so her hand is above her head and to the side. The sun shines on her body and forehead. Her eyes are squinting, and her mouth is half-open. She is either giving a scream or a laugh. She is a playful adolescent, a student at the Catholic mission, and a dancer in her village of Poto-Poto. She seems to find the entire scenario ridiculous. Resistance.

After the failure of the river shoot, Lefebvre went to her village to take photos of Héliani dancing. Photographs are taken of her preparation. A relative applies her makeup. A hand keeps her head from moving. The woman applying the makeup is focused with a subtle contented smile on her face as she rubs her fingers against Héliani's forehead. Héliani is serene and beautiful. Unlike the photo in the tall grass, she is taking this moment seriously. The women are preparing for the celebration to welcome the photographer to their village. He takes pictures of Héliani alone, showing off her makeup. Some of these photos are in *Eve Noire*. Her serious look conveys pride in the love and work that went into applying the traditional makeup. Héliani danced with her sister as people from the village looked on. The girls are hunched over, their legs powerfully moving up and down

La Grand-Poste de Brazzaville

AU VILLAGE DE POTO-POTO

Les bords de l'Oust

Danseuses Linguala au village de Poto-Poto

L'Hymne au Soleil (de la belle Henriette du village de Poto-Poto)

Figs. 2.4–2.6. Pages from Bernard Lefebvre's *Avec de Gaulle en Afrique* that show photographs contextualized with information about how they came to be, the impression of the photographer, and notes about the subject, Héliani. Bernard Lefebvre, *Avec de Gaulle en Afrique* (Luneray: Bertout, 1990), 136–37, 138–39, and 140–41.

against the ground, the energy visible in their bodies through the stillness of the photographs. The photographer describes the costumes and his impressions in his memoir: "Hellani, because that is her name, is a student of the Sisters of the Catholic Mission school, but adheres to the traditions of her tribe and 'does tam-tam' in Poto-Poto after morning mass."[13] Some years later, Lefebvre learned that Héliani was the cover model for *Eve Noire*, and remarked, "My little beauty from Poto-Poto will stay the most beautiful Black Eve from the years 1940–1945."[14] "His" little beauty.

In the context of photographs of Héliani posing in her village, being cared for, and preparing for a celebration, knowing that she was initially approached while she was with her sister creates a new narrative. Lefebrve's memoir is a narrative separated from the archives in which the photographs are kept. The other parts of the book displace the context we imagine Héliani in, or rather, they remind us that colonization is never-ending war. The title page of *Avec de Gaulle en Afrique* includes a single sentence: "Gun is in my strap, but my camera is loaded and ready to shoot." Héliani exists. The viewer decides what is outside of the frame. More men with their colonial gazes? Other dancers? Her family? Or tanks, guns, and military men, also armed and ready to shoot, as those are the images surrounding her and the other young women Lefebvre photographed on his days off. Images of battlefields and military displays in colonial context must be understood against images of colonial subjects living their everyday lives. Every day for these young women likely included encounters with the repressive colonial state. The repressive colonial state created these photographs. That is not what or who Héliani is.

"Hottentot" heirs and life in Paris.

"No neologism can mask the new certainty: the plunge into the chasm of the past is the condition and the source of freedoms."[15] Often, rather than looking into the past, a grand story is latched onto. This becomes the story that determines how we understand swaths of people. The circumstances that surround the life of an individual of note become the circumstances of all those who resemble them. When we look toward the past, we see that just as there is a "Mohamed," there is a "Venus Hottentot."[16] It is unclear if the idea of the Venus Hottentot is the chasm or the condition that makes the chasm possible.

The term *Hottentot* is intimately linked to Saartjie Baartman. As the Venus Hottentot, she was displayed in London and Paris, where she eventually died in the 1820s. The story of her body did not end with her death, though. Georges Cuvier, a French naturalist and zoologist who helped establish the fields of anatomy and paleontology, took her dead body and made a cast. He removed her brain and enlarged labia (which he called the "Hottentot apron"), pickled them, and put them on display along with her skeleton. Her cast was put first in the Garden of Plants, and later, the Jardin d'Acclimatation in Paris.

The story of Baartman is central to how the Black female body is understood in media and scholarship, particularly around contemporary issues of commodification, power, resistance, and embodied experience. Her body is the medium through which the Black female body enters the large cultural landscape of knowledge production. Limited agency, tragic endings, and the white male gaze define the medium. Her existence is what made seeing twelve people on display in a zoo in 1888 so tantalizing; people alive and in the flesh, to be gawked at and interacted with by European families, putting on shows and selling the hierarchy of culture through their perceived inferiority. While their photographs have continued to be circulated through scholarship, their voices have not.

In the summer of 1888, Parisian Thursdays and Sundays were filled with concerts in the Jardin d'Acclimatation, where visitors heard a song based on the traditional music of the strange visitors, a group of *Hottentots*, twelve in total.[17] In addition to the people, five zebras and two ostriches had been brought to Paris to complete the authentic enclosure.[18] Two affective journeys are possible when encountering the people who took part in this exhibition in the photographic archive: either assume the European sentimentality or reject the dominant narrative. Sentimentality renders the group of people in 1888 victims of birth and circumstance. Sentimentality is born from reveling in the "oddity" of their existence and how their bodies became the objects of scientific study, which is shameful and should lead to guilt, but today is detached from the past. We must turn inward to make sense of our feelings.

The next logical step is to fall into solidarity with their suffering through empathy. Rejection of this narrative starts with acknowledging the agency these people (apart from their children) had, rather than focusing on the wound of colonization as something their bodies own. Per Sara Ahmed, "Bringing pain into politics requires we give up the fetish of the wound through different kinds of remembrance. The past is living rather than dead; the past lives in the very wounds that remain open in the present."[19] The archives have more than the photographs. On August 18, 1888, *Le Temps* (Paris), a daily newspaper, ran a story titled "La vie à Paris," an interview by Hugues Le Roux with Mr. Thege, the people trader–cum–translator who brought the group to Paris, and Lisbeth, the matriarch of the group. The following text is my translation of a portion of the interview. The strikethrough is mine as well:[20]

> ~~I have a good friend, former "sergeant" in the Jardin d'Acclimation, who wears a three-medal guard uniform, who, after having done thirty years of excellent police work in the streets of Paris, now yells the dreaded "Move It Along!" to the elephant, to the placid dromedary, to the camel, and the ostrich that runs around the garden with babies riding on its back.~~
>
> ~~So, seeing walls covered with posters announcing the arrival of authentic Hottentots to the Parisian population, I had written to this good fellow.~~
>
> ~~"Let me know," I said to him, "a time that works for me to meet these strangers."~~

~~Since he was forced to swap out his beat copper's cloak for the bottle-green tunic, my old sergeant already offered the hospitality of the turf to Galibis, Araucans, Fuegians, Kalmouks, Eskimos, Red Skins, Lapps, Cynghales, Gauchos, and Ashanti. He is therefore more familiar with the morals of the savage people than the late de la Harpe, Levaillant, Buffon, and other navigators, prose writers, and naturalists, who could not excuse all their lies with the fact that they'd come from afar. Now, my brave sarge made this remark which has its value:~~

~~"When the barometer goes down, the savage curls up."~~

~~I should tell you that since they disembarked from Cape Town, only the few who came in their raincoats have seen them, and then, only to see the Hottentots' unpleasant appearance, which resembled hedgehogs rolled into balls. But the sun of these last few days, which suddenly rose like a ramp, warmed them and ended their sluggishness. They jumped to their feet, they uttered their war cry, swung their kirris, and my faithful sergeant telegraphed me:~~

~~"—Come!"~~

~~The wealthy Parisians who frequent the Jardin d'Acclimatation only in winter and at the dawn of spring cannot imagine the radiant colors of paradise on earth this big farm has on display during the beautiful days of August, when all the beasts wake up and finally come out of their greenhouses and, for an hour, dream of the beautiful sun, of their past freedom. The dogs bark at far-off bitches from their kennel; the battalion of flamingos flutters at the edge of the pool, immobile and alone in their enclosure, their eyes veiled in a ray of sunshine; the white camel dully stomps on the sand, making the same muffled thump as a man shaking the dirt from his shoes before entering his home.~~

~~The Hottentots, like all the savages that have been exhibited, are situated on that great lawn where the procession of Noah's Ark is normally. From a distance, you can see a crowd of black backs, three rows deep, swarming the enclosure; they resemble a swarm of fierce flies on a Queen-Claude. It would take a good hour to approach the rails. But my friend the sergeant knew we were coming; he beckoned me over.~~

~~"You arrived at the right moment," he said, opening the door of the sacred enclosure. "The whole tribe is on parade. Look, to your left, there they are."~~

~~In my line of sight under the sycamores along the gate, I see a dozen unusually shaped and colored people, parading in front of onlookers. My first reaction is to laugh and scream:~~

~~I am a victim of this panorama. It is not possible that these are real life people; the men, maybe; but the women! They seem like what one sees in a funhouse mirror! But no! we are not at the fair: the Jardin d'Acclimatation is a scientific field experience. These naked people are the Hottentots.~~

~~"They are just naked enough," quips a joker in the crowd, "that they can be exhibited without revealing their abundant Hottentot apron!"~~

~~The little Bolbec scarf with large checks that sits under the armpits of women and forces their breasts into a pear shape is a gift from M. Saint-Hilaire; but the kind of loincloth tied around the backs of Hottentots, which drapes down to the backs of their legs above the knee, is a tanned sheepskin, an authentic fashion in their country.~~

~~I ask my comrade the sergeant a question:~~

~~"What are your friends the Hottentots wearing under their sheepskins?"~~

~~"But, sir . . . with all due respect . . . they don't wear anything under their sheepskins. They are generally like that. Even the more than one hundred and fifty doctors of Paris, who came to see us last week, told us that because of the posterior eccentricity of these Hottentots, who are comprised of Namaquas, Karanas, Bushmen, were generally put together, in scientific books, the Great tribe . . ."~~

~~No, I will not be able to tell you, "out of respect," what the one hundred and fifty doctors of Paris called this chubby tribe. Gentlemen of the Faculty, there are ladies here!~~

~~It is necessary—in spite of myself—that I stop at the description of this prodigious profile. A whole Hottentotess is here. She is providentially marked by the characteristic sign of her race. The man, supple, very nervous, very agile, very light, almost spindly, looks like a stand-in for all the savages of the world. It is scarcely enough to notice the petiteness of their eyes, the sparseness of their black hair shorn in tufts, the tremendous distance of the nose, carefully cultivated in infancy by the Hottentot nurses, who carefully sit on the faces of newborns with care. Art here, perfects nature. And, thanks to the "steatopygia," the scientific word for the fat around the buttocks which afflicts, or if one likes better, beautifies these ladies, only a few sessions of face sitting are needed to make the nose of a Hottentot absolutely invisible when you look at their face from the side.~~

~~Have you ever wondered how these wretched savages are hired and brought with arms and baggage from all the ends of the earth? With the "bamboulas" that Barnum exhibits in circuses, we are suspicious. I told you formerly how fake Zulus were meticulously fabricated in a London shop, with ordinary nègres with a bit of color applied to their skin, and~~

appropriated tattoos. In the Jardin d'Acclimation one has, to be reassured, the certificate of origin authenticated by one hundred and fifty doctors of Paris. This tribe comes from Bushmen country.

"But how on earth, comrade, did anyone persuade these savages to come and see the Eiffel Tower?"

"Ask the interpreter who brought them," the sergeant responded. "Here he is."

I find myself face to face with a character of about thirty years, vigorous like a fairground showman, who has a hooked nose, a tan complexion, a capped eyelid, and, in general, the build of a Piedmont digger. This Mr. Thege is from Hamburg. In his youth, he was what in the ports of the Ocean we call a "merchant of men." He ran a mariners' employment office. At twenty-five, he was bitten by the travel bug. He sailed for southern Africa. From these distant lands he has trafficked a little bit of everything.

"I have succeeded," he said in bad English mixed with Dutch and German, "in taking these people through the fat matriarch whom you see there, and whom I will present to you in a bit, old Lisbeth. I first proposed a trip of the city. I brought them hesitantly to the railway and took them by the reins into the train cars. In Cape Town, we took advantage of their bewilderment and put them on a boat. I say "we" because I had a colleague who has since left us. He was an adventurous boy who had gone out penniless and came back with pockets full of diamonds. As soon as we arrived in Paris, he ran to the jewelers to sell his treasure. He was given a large sum of gold; it made him lose his head: he disappeared."

I wanted to know what profit these savages could get out of their European tour, and I questioned Mr. Thege about it. I'm sure he told me the truth, because old Lisbeth, questioned separately, told me the same numbers.

"I have promised," replied the interpreter, "a pound and ten shillings to women, and two pounds to the men a month; but that's not a tenth of their earnings. Visitors give them a lot of money. Lisbeth earns fifty francs every Sunday, by twirling in her loincloth. She is a very talented old woman. She has almost as much influence over the group as Jacob, the chief, since we've been on the road.

Jacob, the big boy you see parading around with that stick, the "kirris," which is used by the Hottentots along with pebbles and arrows. Jacob is a very skilled hunter. From a hundred steps away, he can hit a goal the size of a penny with any stone he touches. He is considered a great hunter in his village. He was the recipient, a few years ago, of a very enviable distinction that is conferred on valiant men during their strange ceremonies. The hero who kills a lion, an elephant, or a buffalo, lies in the middle of his hut, and all the elders of the tribe come and pour water on him . . ."

Shall I really tell you how the elders of the tribune watered the wretched Jacob?

Remember the bad joke that Gargantua played on Parisians from the towers of Notre-Dame: "He was bathed by one hundred and sixty people, not counting women and little children." The Hottentot warrior leaves the ceremony a majestic person, following this immersive baptism. The warrior is respected, their orders are no longer up for discussion. Thus, even in Paris, Jacob's authority remains undisputed: every morning he designates a man who will cook for the day. This man gets up at the stroke of six, splits wood, and heats a large pot of water outside in which he mixes, in almost equal proportions, coffee and salt. Each member of the tribe consumes a liter and a half of this mixture. It has essence of their own food. It's not on par with the good termite and grasshopper soup they make in their own country; but, on a journey like this, one must be content with little.

The imposed regularity of meals is a novelty for these savages. Carefree, lazy, stupid, men and women, endure endless fasts with tobacco and brandy. They are content to tighten the strap that supports their loin cloth. When their bellies, eventually, scream too loudly, they form a band of hunters, go hunting, and, as the game abounds, soon down a big animal that is dismembered on the spot and devoured half-raw.

Mr. Thege saw five Hottentots eat a big ewe, three porcupines, four lizards and snakes, not to mention moles and field mice, in less than an hour.

"And how do your savages feel about the stay in Paris?"

"At first, sir, they were delighted with the curiosity of the people who came to see them. They danced happily and sang while clapping their hands. Now, they ask me every day: 'When will we return to our country?' They were very worried about one of their group members who had an illness and almost died from chest inflammation. The doctors ordered his transportation to the hospital, but he begged with so many tears to not be separated from his comrades, that he should be looked after here in the dormitory. Jacob said: 'If he leaves, we want to go with him.' By the way, sir, Lisbeth understands English, so you can interview her yourself."

Then Mr. Thege called: "Lisbeth! Lisbeth!"[21]

I imagine her approaching Mr. Thege making the same face she is making in a photo where she is seated with a family who were brought to Paris

Fig 2.7. *From left to right:* Jacob, Mina, Lisbeth, Esther, and unnamed daughter. In the archive, the title of this image is *Hottentots. Types ethniques,* and the names of the individuals are unlisted. The album is located under the name of the collection and the collection owner. Image reproduced with permission from BnF, Société de Géographie.

with her. Lisbeth stares straight ahead with her arms crossed over her stomach, flanked with the older daughter and the patriarch of the family on one side, and the mother with her infant daughter in her arms to the right and slightly behind, with a face that says, "don't fuck with us."

Lisbeth is big. She takes up space. While the Parisians saw her only as a spectacle, she was a respected tribe member. And to be very clear, this group was there to work. What she was not there for was Jacob's foolishness. When there was a shift in the weather and the sun shone on, Le Roux spoke with Lisbeth in an interview:

LE ROUX Hello Lisbeth, I said, are you happy to see the sunshine return?

LISBETH I am always happy, she responded, when the gentleman gives me a coin.

LE ROUX I'll give you a coin in a moment, Lisbeth, if you would take a moment to talk to me. How old are you?

LISBETH I am old.

LE ROUX Do you have children?

LISBETH Ten. Five are still with me. A panther ate one.

LE ROUX Are you married?

LISBETH Widowed.[22]

Lisbeth's interviews always ended with her finding something to say about Jacob, even if he *was* the chief of the group. When Le Roux asked Lisbeth about the group's thoughts on the women that come to see them, Jacob, according to Lisbeth, said, "If he didn't have a wife and kids, he would really like to get married to them."[23]

Lisbeth was able to give a voice to the group. A *Gaulois: Littéraire et Politique* article, "Les Hottentots à Paris," from July of 1888, mentions that they had been baptized by missionaries, which is why they have English names. This same article speaks of a troubling incident in which Jacob asked Lisbeth, who was seated far away from the rails of the enclosure, to come and speak to people who had given them some money. She didn't want to move. The two of them violently fought and yelled at each other. Jacob slapped Lisbeth. Lisbeth gave in and reluctantly came up and spoke to the visitors.

An article about a month later, from August 2, 1888, in *Le Voleur Illustré: Cabinet de Lecture Universel*, spoke out against the inhumanity of putting "savages" on display as they were, and took the interaction between Lisbeth and Jacob, and her protest that instigated their fight, as proof that this practice was wrong and that the people in these shows did not wish to be shown in enclosures. The article was, as stated, an initial attempt to "protest very vigorously against the very principles of these human expositions."[24]

There were others who also tried to use the group to shift the narratives and myths that surrounded the Khoikhoi people. The group was extensively photographed by Prince Roland Bonaparte. In explaining his sponsorship and donation of the photographs to the Société de Géographie in 1889, he stated that he had "given the congress [of the geographic society] the photographs [he] took of the Hottentots, which will permit for the naturalist to destroy the current legends of the origins of this race."[25] This is further implied as an area of focus by the article "La stéatopygie des Hottentotes du Jardin d'acclimatation," in the proceedings of a conference that the Société de Médecine held in the Garden of Acclimation to examine steatopygia and the *Hottentot apron*. Despite the subject, the article starts with physician Paul Topinard implying that there is no *Hottentot* and that the people called

Fig 2.8. Lisbeth, standing, likely in the enclosure. In the archive, the title of this image is *[African Woman]*, ca. 1888. The photographer is identified as Prince Roland Napoleon Bonaparte (French, 1858–1924). Courtesy of the J. Paul Getty Museum, Los Angeles. getty .edu/art/collection /object/107NWF.

by this name are a diverse group of crossed and mixed races.[26] This article contains one photograph, a picture of Lisbeth, nude, from behind. It also gives the names of two more women, though there are no photographs of them: Maria and Esther.

At the end of the interview with Le Roux, Lisbeth is asked if she would want to stay in Paris. She says no, because it is too cold, to which Le Roux says it is more beautiful than where she is from. She asked him if he knew her country. He replies no, but he is basing his comments on what Thege told him about the barren land she came from. Lisbeth, with a reserved smile, responds: "I know well that the country is barren. Those who live on the other side of the moon killed the country. But when Nâno (the ill

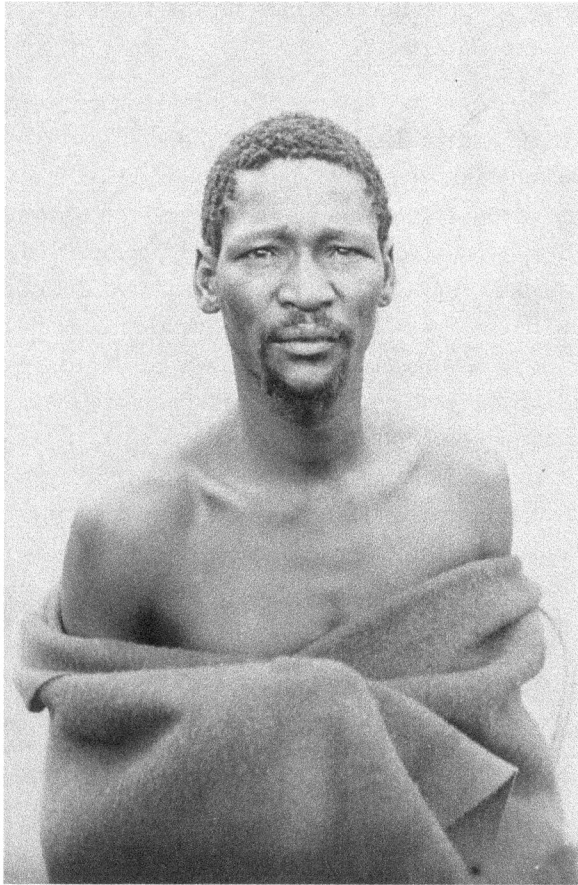

Fig 2.9. Portrait of Jacob Mailie. In the archive, the title of this image is *Jacob Mailie, 34 ans,* ca. 1888. The photographer is identified as Prince Roland Napoleon Bonaparte (French, 1858–1924). Courtesy of the J. Paul Getty Museum, Los Angeles. getty .edu/art/collection /object/107NVJ.

member of their group) returns he will be cured. When will we leave for our country, Mr. Thege?"

Jacob agreed to be interviewed for *Gil Blas* on July 21, 1888, in an article titled "Chez les Hottentots," in exchange for some cigars. He remarks:

I did not want to leave my country; I was afraid they wanted to take me to fatten me up first and then eat me. But I let them persuade me, and I don't regret it. At home, we had to fish or hunt all day; here, all I do is have fun and toss around my assegai. I eat everything I want to, I smoke tobacco. I'd be very happy if it were just a bit warmer and if we were given a bit more brandy. But when my time here is up, I'll buy brandy and take it home, and I'll spend a lot of time doing nothing with the money I've earned. And do you know what I would do if I had a lot of gold? I would take some of your women and put them on exhibit on the grass there, for our warriors. I swear to you that they would be a novel success.[27]

The digital archives are a cache of information, interviews, names, photographs, and studies that allow the individuals who made up this group to be known differently. For instance, there is an image of the young girl in the various digital repositories that has been reproduced in many books. "Betty, 9 years old," is written on the photograph. The album that shows her with her family is not commonly reproduced. The misinformation written on the easy-to-find photographs spreads. Her name is not Betty, and she is not nine years old. She is Mina Mailie, six years old, daughter of Jacob and Esther, who came to Paris with her parents and her three-month-old sister who had not yet been named.

Though Mina was not interviewed, a moment of her life was seen as remarkable enough to warrant being included at the end of the article from *Le Gaulois:*

> As we were going, we heard screams: it was Mina, the little Hottentot girl, who was playing loudly with a child dressed in all white, the daughter of a lady who came to see this curiosity.... These two children seemed to have a lot of fun and got along very well. The two races.[28]

The narratives of suffering and dehumanization can be accepted as the most important aspect of the experience these people had. The other option is to expand the collective knowledge of their experiences, acknowledging that suffering and dehumanization were part of the context—but not all of it. In reading the words of Lisbeth and Jacob, and in studying their experience, I cannot help but return to Fanon:

> Locked in this suffocating reification, I appealed to the Other so that his liberating gaze, gliding over my body suddenly smoothes [*sic*] of rough edges would give me back the lightness of being I thought I had lost, and talking me out of the world put me back in the world. But just as I get to the other slope I stumble, and the Other fixes me with his gaze, his gestures and attitude, the same way you fix a preparation with a dye. I lost my temper, demand an explanation.... Nothing doing. I explode. Here are the fragments put together by another me.[29]

In the instance where Jacob and Lisbeth fight, the translator gets involved and reminds Lisbeth why they are there. Jacob reminds her of the money they are making. Together, they portray a fighting Lisbeth at the moment

Fig 2.10. Portrait of Mina. In the archive, the title of this image is *Betty, fillette hotentotte (Hottentot girl), 9 ans.* ca 1888. The photographer is identified as Prince Roland Napoleon Bonaparte (French, 1858–1924). Courtesy of the J. Paul Getty Museum, Los Angeles. getty.edu/art/collection/object/107NW7.

of her trying to explode. It is too soon, and too late. She is already there. From Edith Stein:

> What became, was lived, and is finished sinks back into the stream of the past. We leave it behind us when we step into a new experience; it loses its primordiality but remains the "same experience." First it is alive and then dead, but not first non-psychic and then psychic.[30]

To explode the archive, in a Fanonian sense, into something that can be built anew allows for the creation of different futures with names, words, utterances, confrontations, and relationships.

I am omitting certain things. They are the already-known facts that confirm the inherited assumptions. All the people had clothed and anthropological nude portraits done, including Mina. There are records and write-ups of their public medical exams, where spectators watched doctors examine all the things that made them too abundant to be understood as fully human by the Parisian crowds. To focus, though, on just the moment that speaks to the complete exploitation of these people, imagined as vulnerable and without agency, is to deny their moments of resistance and agency. The narrative they are placed in has to be reconciled with their excursions to the Eden Théâtre, where they were featured in a show and were allowed to watch the bit of the performance they were not a part of. They did the same when they went to "Théâtre Robert-Houdin to see the prestidigitation tricks," an event that was reported in the *New York Herald, European Edition,* "Stage Gossip" section on September 15, 1888.[31] I imagine how mischievous Mina—who whenever photographed with her father looks like she was just scolded—was delighted.

I have so many questions about Mina and how she experienced and remembered this brief childhood excursion to Paris. I wonder what she felt when her photographs were taken. I wonder how often Mina looked at the feet of two of the women staring directly into the camera, her mother and baby sister barely visible in the background. Her little body tries to mimic the way a woman should stand (which is with the left foot a bit ahead of the right one, which is very slightly angled out, as it were). I wonder how she looked when she found her own stance, like theirs, but with a difference. Was Paris a lasting memory that she spoke about for the rest of her life? All my thoughts about Mina continue the flattening of her being, arrested at age six with her family in Paris. She was older than my great-grandmother. The group had supplementary performances in settings other than the Garden of Acclimation. They took part in the Cirque d'Eté. And before their departure they were part of a performance at the Folies-Bergère. They went from Paris to London. Did having the gift of language among the English allow Lisbeth to feel freer during that brief passage?

I have to grapple with her digital afterlife. I found these pictures and articles in the digital archives of the French National Library and the J. Paul Getty's free educational content. I looked for more pictures that were digitized, through similar image searches. I found two postcards, a predigital way to share interesting photographs, at the website humanzoos .net. I haven't found these postcards anywhere else. The digitized postcards are watermarked with the name of the website and the name of the site's owner, Clemens Radauer. They are photographs of items he has collected, his own private museum that can be visited digitally. The collection puts the images back into an enclosure, a named man, a human zoo, and nameless people,

Fig 2.11. Mina, looking down at the feet of Maria and Bebye, with Esther and the Maile baby standing in the background. In the archive, the title of this image is *Hottentots. Types ethniques.* Image reproduced with permission from BnF, Société de Géographie.

and on the page: "1888 Jardin Zoologique d'Acclimatation—Hottentots." One of the postcards features the Mailie family, the other, the whole group. I haven't seen these photographs anywhere else. The images, when clicked on, are very clear. The photograph of the baby is the only one I've seen in which her face is visible. She is adorable. Mina, as always, looks like she has just been scolded. Esther looks older, and so tired. Jacob looks tired as well. Others from the group are in the background.

I look at the page, and I wish that the images from magazine, postcards, and jounals had been contextualized with something more. The material, absent the words or the curator, creates the same white, empathetic gaze; seeing these images here rather than in a library's digital repository makes different things stand out, and the images are displayed in such a way that the viewer performs a particular reading without explanatory text. The page for the 1888 Jardin Zoologique d'Acclimation displays a booklet that can't be browsed first, then sees the photographs/postcards, and ends with the illustrations (figure 2.12). I missed that the price to see the original

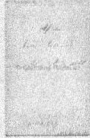

Fig 2.12. Screenshot of "1888 Jardin Zoologique d'Acclimatation— Hottentots," Human Zoos, accessed November 6, 2022. https://humanzoos .net/?page_id=3034.

exhibition was five centimes, but because the first page of the booklet is the first thing I see, I focus in on it a bit more than I had when it showed up in a Gallica search. When I get through the infographics featuring vignettes with tiny descriptions, I feel a bit undone. I always want these things to be more. There isn't enough here for me to form a feeling beyond the immediate breathing out. The photographs only mean more because I know a bit about who I am seeing.

The website humanzoos.net isn't the same as *Human Zoos: The Invention of the Savage*. It is not trying to recreate something that existed. The home page welcomes visitors with the following:

Welcome to humanzoos.net—the first online archive on human zoos.

This homepage [*sic*] aims to be a guide for people interested in the phenomenon of human zoos, especially the visual remnants. The core of this archive is the *Collection Radauer* consisting of over 3000 postcards, photographs, publicity materials, newspaper articles and other items linked to the exhibition of "exotic" people in Europe and the USA.

It's not the zoo; it is its visual remnants, the ones a single person, Radauer, can physically touch and own. As the object of interest is this type of material, it highlights the afterlife of his physical objects as they are used to illustrate the oppression inherent in these practices. He and I are both collectors, tracing the afterlives of these happenings. He just happens to collect the physical objects. I follow the traces through their digital movement. We have both written ourselves into this story. I've not found any of the other postcards and never received responses from archives that might have known more about them. I am left to imagine what else is lost or hidden in different places.

Another aspect of the digital afterlife of images is the research. Having access to images through the Getty's Open Content program is a wonderful thing that allows for deeper exploration and scholarship. Because it is free, easier-to-find, high-resolution versions images can be downloaded in an instant, and they are more likely to continue to make their way into new scholarship. Some of the photographs in this book are reproduced with their required captions. Citationality continues to perpetuate limitations on understanding and contextualizing what we are seeing. The description of Lisbeth's nameless photo from the website is described as a "Somewhat older African woman with unusually large calves standing in front of giraffe and various other skins, with her head wrapped in checkered cloth and draped at the waist with a couple of different animal skins." Mina's description offers less, "African girl seated on a chair wearing three beaded necklaces and fur piece." Jacob's captions are "African male with mustache and beard seated, facing frontally, wrapped from mid-chest down in blanket," and "African male with mustache and beard seated, in profile, wrapped from mid-chest down in blanket." These photographs leave people nameless (Lisbeth) or with the inaccurate caption (Mina as Betty), as the requirement for using them is to use the given caption.

The metadata lists Africa as the place where the photos were created even though the photographs were taken in Paris. There are so many blanks; there is so much misinformation. There is no way to discover what we don't know. We are left with just our feelings and our cultural understandings of the context of the photographs. Leaning into empathy is a shortcut. The digital access to archives lets us know that there is more to these photos; our ability to search and find linked information and artifacts is a marvel. It would have taken so much more time if the only way to engage with these things were in-person, from archive to archive. Metadata reveals the broader world that Mina, Jacob, and Lisbeth existed in.

A favorite find of mine, from the clippings about the group, appeared in the October 19, 1888, edition of the *Chicago Tribune*, in a section called "For the Ladies," titled "Direction for Women Smokers: Rules for Their Guidance Prepared by a Parisian Expert." This segment ends with the following:

> The guide might have added an injunction to the fumeuses which would be well worth their attention had she said: "Go and see the Hottentot women smoke in the Jardin des Plantes." The three or four brown skinned beauties from the Bush who are now exhibiting themselves daily to the Parisians have a way of inhaling and emitting tobacco smoke which would be worthy of emulation of the most artistically disposed Parisian fumeuse. It is true that the Hottentot ladies smoke big cigars which they beg from visitors, and that they do not disdain the short black pipe of clay, but they have a fine way of manipulating the numerous cigarettes which are also given to them gratis, and they emit the smoke from their rather wide nostrils in a perfectly natural and graceful manner.[32]

People saw beauty in the way smoke made their breath visible, as it took advantage of their unique features. It's an unexpected moment of movement, where those who paid to see them recognizing the beauty of the women that was not captured in photos.

I wonder if their descendants know that these interviews and photographs exist. The "them" on the other side of empathy, the "they" who feel

Fig 2.13. Photograph of the group brought to Paris in 1888. Speculative names (*from left to right*): Maria, Elisa Rooi, April Much, Bebye Rooi [?], Jacob Mailie, Mina, Esther holding a three-month-old baby girl, Lisbeth, Betsy [?], Jeremiah Beity, and the back of an unnamed and unimportant European man. In the archive, the title of this image is *Hottentots. Types ethniques.* Image reproduced with permission from BnF, Société de Géographie.

for the "Other"; both are and are not me. The past demands confrontation as it mingles with an imagined past, the "us" that sees today becomes part of "them" as we rewrite and reconnect the archive. Showing the moments of exploitation and expectedness in context does not take away the power of other moments. It makes them stronger, because we have a glimpse into what could have been had the structures of oppression not shaped how people in the Black diaspora came to be understood. To do this type of work requires speculation, where speculation is understood to be a way of seeing specters and a form of introspection. How do I make this world worth living in, and how do we create a more just and inclusive future if we do not write the other aspects of the past into being? How can I look toward loved ones, ancestors, and kinfolk in the past if all I acknowledge is their suffering and never their voices, which are buried in translation and problematic structures of knowing?

By cross-referencing the digital archives, we can better speculate about the names of most of the people in the group photograph. Jacobus Much (or Huch) is not pictured:[33]

I want to create new worlds for the descendants and kinfolk of the future. This is, as Saidiya Hartman states, a small attempt at a "Dream . . . for existing otherwise."[34] In the otherwise, and in the snippets of their lives in Paris as found in the archives, understandings come into being. While Jacob saw the experience as a release from obligations and reveled in being a spectacle in a fabricated village behind a chain, Lisbeth saw it for what it was: a cage. A cage that she denounced at any opportunity she could, just as she used every opportunity to denounce Jacob and how he was acting. Afterall, Jacob was, in modern terms, a fuckboy.

3: New media and emerging technology will kill us all, though.

The present technological system amplifies the power structure onto which it is grafted.
—Ursula Franklin, *Will Women Change Technology or Will Technology Change Women?*

The aspiration of our time for wholeness, empathy, and depth of awareness is a natural adjunct of electric technology. The age of mechanical and industry that preceded us found vehement assertion of private outlook the natural mode of expression. Every age has its favorite model of perception and knowledge that is inclined to prescribe for everybody and everything.
—Marshall McLuhan, "Understanding Media: The Extensions of Man"

Technology, with its orientation toward the past when directly engaging with the social production of empathy, is a carceral imaginary.[1] *Carcer* refers to either a jail or a confined space, especially at the beginning of something; it is connected to where people were held before performances. This root allows us to think about technology beyond the typical confines of the carceral imaginary as defined by Ruha Benjamin. In addition to the active participation in the prison-industrial complex, technology attempts to contain an end user in a confined and imagined space by limiting the ways a user can engage. This is done by designing technology for specific contexts and with limited affordances. It happens before an end user is allowed to engage performatively with the technology through a coded script. When technology has reached its pinnacle, the person on the other side need not really exist for there to be meaningful technological engagement. Technology imprisons certain bodies in their suffering and positions that suffering as the beginning and end.

Augmenting hyperreality.

The argument that empathy leads to more ethical action or connection is moot in the digital context as the mediated representation of the person on the other side of technology is not the actual person. It is not even related to the actual person. It is a past image of a person who may or may not still be living, positioned to ensure that the walls of imagination around them are limited. The act of putting on an extended reality headset in your own environment and taking it off or holding up a phone to get more information that otherwise would not be there reinforces this dynamic. It is what Benjamin calls an "act of discriminatory design," as it "normalizes racial hierarchies—not as an ideological aberration from business-as-usual, but as an economic imperative that is built into the machine."[2] Augmented and virtual reality normalize violent colonial imagery in the imagination and experience of the absent Other. It takes the carceral imaginary a step further by insisting that the world is a prison, and only the virtual or augmented world can set you free.

The current augmented hyperreality created by high-definition representational technologies is being led by virtual reality (VR) and augmented reality (AR). They, of course, are not the first; telephones, radio, photographs, film, television, all prepared us to step technologically into VR or AR overlays. Ursula Franklin explores this in *The Real World of Technology*:

> The images create new realities with intense emotional components. In the spectators they create a sense of "being there," of being in some sense a participant rather than an observer. There is a powerful illusion of presence in places and occasions where the spectators, in fact, are not and have never been. . . . The selective fragment that becomes a story . . . [is] chosen to highlight particular events. The selection is usually intended to attract and retain the attention of an audience. Consequently, the unusual has preference over the usual. The faraway that cannot be assessed through experience has preference over the near that can be experienced directly.[3]

Reality is already virtual and augmented because it is full of inherent bias and imagined encounters with the Other. Despite the illusion of true participation, the tools of extended reality foreclose reciprocity. The illusion of choice is enough to blur the fact that these technologies isolate and force people down predetermined paths. In the new hyperreality machines, walls disappear. The human senses this lack of boundaries without a means of mutually benefiting, because the other side of the tool is no longer a person. As an object in a technological environment, humans are forced into virtual boxes and deep-dives into personal emotions (both positive and negative).

Because of the one-sidedness of all of these technologies, creators and early adopters are desperately trying to rationalize and justify the new contours of society they are attempting to create, which are really just reified contours of the same old society. Supposedly, technologies will make the world better for everyone and not only the owners of the companies who make the machines and the software or own the gates that allow users to go through a paywall after paying a toll. The business solution, because it is big business, is empathy. Benjamin states, "Empathy makes businesses grow. In the first quarter of 2016, venture capitalists invested almost $1.2 billion in VR technologies, almost 50% more than in the previous quarter."[4] Going back to the discourse, the money guides how we think about these "empathy machines." We accept empathy as "lawful good," even as we place technology companies between "lawful evil" and "chaotic evil."[5] We engage with the constructed experiences knowing they are made with biases, just as all algorithms and all other technology and emergent forms of remediation are made.[6]

It is generally accepted that empathy is the "eat the poor and marginalized" approach rather than the "eat the rich and powerful" approach to experience. We are not asked to jump into an intense boardroom meeting as the CEO of a Fortune 500 company, followed by a sojourn at the country club for a round of golf and a shopping trip to add a luxury car to our growing collection. Instead, anyone with a headset is invited to become homeless. Empathy machines, then, rather than designing a better, more human future, seem to train us to increase our capacity for accepting the misery and suffering all around us.

"Becoming Homeless," a VR experience created by Stanford's Virtual Human Interaction Lab, premiered at the 2017 Tribeca Film Festival. The experience allows users with access to VR headsets costing hundreds of dollars, rooms with ample amounts of empty space, and powerful computers to "become" homeless in a matter of minutes:

The Fundamental Attribution Error, as coined by Stanford Psychologists, describes how we blame others when bad things happen to them, but blame the external situations when bad things happen to us. There is a misconception that losing one's home is due to who you are and the choices you make. "Becoming Homeless: A Human Experience" seeks to counter this irrational tendency.

In this immersive virtual reality experience from Stanford University's Virtual Human Interaction Lab, spend days in the life of someone who can no longer afford a home. Interact with your environment to attempt to save your home and to protect yourself and your belongings as you walk in another's shoes and face the adversity of living with diminishing resources.[7]

You start in an apartment. The mood is set with foreboding music and radio reports on the state of the economy. The narrator speaks directly into your headset and makes the following suggestion: sell six things in your apartment before you are evicted. You look down at your desk and see an eviction notice, documents with lots of red markings and an oversized "No!," a coffee cup and an empty paper plate (figure 3.1). Perhaps you'll make enough to pay rent. The money, of course, is not enough. You now live in your car below an underpass. The police show up. You sell the car because you can't pay for the citation tickets. Congratulations! You now qualify for a free bus pass.

You ride the bus to stay warm and out of the elements. You are in a mini game. You have to protect your bag and avoid being harassed. Two other people are on the bus, one is after your bag and the other is a serial harasser of homeless people. Good luck. You won't win. The music won't stop. Now there are other homeless people on the bus. Stare at them. A homeless person's oral history starts when you look at the person. They tell you how they became homeless. The music does not stop. After listening to each story, a new layer of music starts, a simple piano tune, to create a feeling of something for these people because more than being in their shoes, you embody their experience. The narrator assures you that encountering people in this way helps fight stereotypes. Take off your headset. You are still in your empty room. The total experience lasted under eight minutes. The music never stopped.

Constructed experiences need an audience to be meaningful. These experiences all have two stories for a person who goes through them: one is a description of what the experience was, who you pretend to be, the objects

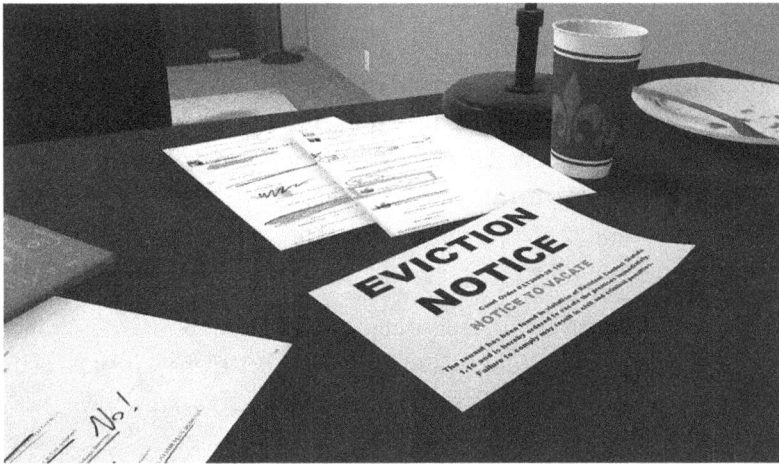

Fig 3.1. Screenshot from "Deep Empathy," Teach AI training survery, part of a joint project of the MIT Media Lab's Scalable Cooperation and UNICEF Innovation. Last accessed on November 6, 2022. deepempathy.mit.edu/survey.

you interact with, the mood, and the technical aspects. The other is the "me" story, where the Other is replaced with the self. Both stories need to be talked about to have an impact. In this sense, the experiencer of VR in which one suddenly undergoes the suffering "speaks not only for but literally in place of" a person who is actually suffering.[8] The ability to own the experience is tied to the long history of subjugations that saw people completely lose agency and ownership of their own lives and life stories. Being homeless digitally does not allow a viewer to connect to a whole other person and their lived experience of the circumstances and inequality responsible for the systemic failures that led to their homelessness. There is no possibility for a dialogue with or an actual person to speak back because there are no homeless people in becoming homeless. The need for firsthand (albeit VR) experience to create a sense of empathy speaks to the need to care only for the immediate rather than for past suffering. When the past is lost and not accounted for, the suffering carries forward and falls into the void. The suffering becomes a state of madness, delirium, or some other mode of being outside of reason. Groups on the margins who have been excluded from society are often described in terms related to their ability to be part of the world and society now. The homeless person is "crazy" just as the Black person is "threatening."

An article shared on the Virtual Human Interaction site titled "Virtual Reality Perspective-Taking Increases Cognitive Empathy for Specific Others" is based on lab study where undergraduate students pretended to be undergraduate students in virtual reality. The students were either paid $100 or not paid and given extra credit in a course. The type of empathy they spent the most time on (getting the experiencer to attach to their avatar) has more to do with physical mirroring than with the deep emotional work troubling VR experiences like "Becoming Homeless" attempts to force onto an experiencer. Even with regard to physical mirroring, their own conclusion states the following:

> Empathy is important for positive human interaction and has been shown in previous research to be associated with prosocial behavior. VRPT is an exercise which uses virtual reality technology to get an individual to take the perspective of someone else, and in other research has been shown to increase prosocial behavior. It has been expected that an increase in empathy is the underlying mechanism for this increase in prosociality, but no previous research has rigorously demonstrated this. Here, we find that VRPT can be used to increase target-specific perspective-taking in individuals. This increase is moderated by the individual's sense of "presence," or how immersed in the virtual environment they report feeling. We do not demonstrate that VRPT increases prosocial behavior as measured through behavioral games.[9]

The question of space and time with both VR and AR cause difficulty in understanding how they affect the transmission of knowledge. Media should be understood through how suited they are to transportation.[10] Both of these media do not allow for the transportation of information because only the person (the viewing subject) is being transported. Further, these technologies assume transportation should be without seams and, thus, all-encompassing. Technologies mimic or create a hyperreal experience of the natural environment.

Determining whether these media are biased toward time and space seems like an impossibility. They are stuck in the time and space of their cultural production. Previous media were designed to be seen in similar ways by people in either different locations or different times. These technological tools are designed to bring the past forward as a replacement for actual reality. A question I keep coming back to is, What is the medium of VR and AR? Is it the body? The device? The content? When Chris Milk changed the name of VRSE to "Within" in June of 2016, he wrote a *Medium* post to explain the decision. In his post, he explained the decision by saying that "vr eliminates the need for external frames. For the first time, the medium is no longer outside us, but within us. The paint is human experience, and the canvas is our consciousness. The idea of an externalized medium ceases to exist."[11]

Virtual reality is an extension of emotions, and augmented reality is an extension of cultural biases. If the medium of vr is the body, and if ar is a technological overlay of the biases of the world, these new and emerging technologies (when we understand them as media) disappear the self, which becomes an Other within the experience. ar makes the world, as medium, incomplete. These tools incomprehensibly destabilize reality. The lack of boundaries disables one's ability to turn away. The thing being experienced continues forward on its own. These technologies answer the question of how people become posthuman; bodies are lost in a sea of computer-generated information. Senses are hijacked and directed at unreality. Judgment and emotions remain. Rather than the technological object being ephemeral, the human is. In this sea of feelings and constructed false worlds, feelings are extended beyond comprehension. A belief that the produced feelings are genuinely what the Other feels is normalized by the hold empathy has on our current moment. Having feelings is not empathy.

Empathy emergence-y.

With emerging technologies and new media, the past is moving forward at an ever-increasing speed and scale, forcing continued dehumanization and distancing. Is it any wonder, then, that all the bad that comes with the new toys and tools for "connecting" is seen only as a failure of empathy? It is worse than a failure. Empathy that has lost its other side, the human part of the interaction, completely. As Benjamin states in *Race after Technology*, there is a "growing discourse around technology and *empathy* (rather than equity or justice)."[12] Like all discourses, to enter the *empathy* conversation, one must be conversant in the terms of use. Empathy, in the technological discourse, is an inherently human trait that can be cultivated and grown, so that an individual has a more positive and personal reaction or response to the Other. Empathy is universally good, and attempting to expand our capacity for it will lead to our becoming better humans. To not have empathy is a sign of personal failure.

Technology, with all its unfixable problems, then, can be remedied if a false sense of humanization is built into it by aligning *technology* with the culturally profitable notion of *empathy* (and empathy expansion, discussed as an increased empathetic response). That is to say, empathy has become part of today's electronic revolution. As James W. Carey and John J. Quirk argue, "The promotion of the illusion of an 'electronic revolution' borders on complicity by intellectuals in the myth-making of the electric complex itself."[13] I do not wish to be complicit. I am stating it plainly: I am leaving the discourse to the best of my ability and shifting the conversation. I accept that empathy is a real thing in as much as it is culturally constructed, technically produced, and socially and electronically reproduced. There is a conversation that needs to be had before we take the notion of empathy as good and the marriage of empathy and technology as worthwhile for critical engagement. The conversation requires rethinking what emerging technologies are and examining what work empathy and technology are doing together.

There are no solutions or actions in empathy, just as there is no better world in technology. If the machines are always at fault, electricity is the cure and the promise. If that promise is a failure as well, move the barometer to people. The onus to make new and emerging forms of technology live up to their promise of productivity and utopian dreams is on the individual.[14] The focus is on the individual's scripted, normalized, mediated, and approved affective response to technology, its content, and its economic power. Emergent technologies exist in relation to capital and continually mask or defer the suffering of those with more power, while providing a safe way to consume the suffering of the Other-as-object. Thus, the subject of technologically mediated empathy is not the human, but the suffering itself.

Technoliberalism, defined by Neda Atanasoski and Kalindi Vora as the "political alibi of present-day racial capitalism," does not need a human on the other side to create an empathetic response.[15] The impact of the experience is not on the people who are transformed into technological objects or content but on what can be achieved in society outside of that person or those people to make mainstream society feel better about itself. The ability to fluently use emerging and new technologies defines groups. Groups become us or them, forward or backward, primitive or civilized based on their technological agility. The past determines who is allowed to be fully human today and the contours of dehumanization for sorting. It determines who, collectively, will be cared for and who, collectively, will suffer and deserves to suffer. The difference created by today's technology is the speed and efficiency of the suffering, aided by technology and a gamified experience across platforms and format, including drone-based combat.

Technology carries affective biases and brings society not to the future but back to the past masquerading as the future. In this way, technology annihilates the possibility of another side, a side beyond the "I" of experience. Society without technology does not exist. We are in an age of continual "technological emergence." The smallest screens, like those in head-mounted displays, create the illusion of existing in a void that can be filled only with VR. Artificial intelligence (AI) and machine learning turn more and more devices into advanced input-output machines, calculators to factor all the questions in the world if we input the right data set, which can experience a curated version of Others that is supposedly the best version. And we are all data. Something as personal as your face has been reduced to a data point, cataloged through a facial recognition system independent of human intervention. Social media feeds the system.

We emerge as ourselves, always anticipating "me today, version 2.0." High-definition, real-time doom-scrolling makes sure the endless suffering of the world is constantly in our data-filled faces to the point that we don't have time to do anything but enjoy it in horror. Guilt? Forget it! We are told that technological progress is better for everyone and that technologies are all tools for empathy and connection, which is really a way of saying it is up to you to do the work to humanize the Others you encounter, knowing some of these Others are bots. We take in a firehose of information and emerging technology, from our fridges to smart water bottles, smart speakers, and wireless headphones, all named so we can find them through Bluetooth and wireless networks. Even if we are not social robots, we are being programmed as though we are.[16]

In responding to a symposium on hot and cool and how these concepts relate to emerging media, Marshall McLuhan said, "We have been through enough revolutions to know every medium of communication is a unique art form which gives salience to one set of human possibilities at the expense of another set. Each medium of expression profoundly modifies human sensibility in mainly unconscious and unpredictable ways."[17] Prosocial behavior, driven by technology, depends on empathy as a pure form of communication despite the extensive mediation it requires. The inability to connect across technology is, as the saying goes, a feature, not a bug. The dream of the technological future is a dream about replacing the need for others altogether, not a dream about genuine connection and being with others. Technological ideologies are based on the ability of those in power to dictate who successfully speaks up and speaks out. Those in power use technology to direct society's feelings.

If the general equation for empathy =

past + self + other

The general equation for technology =

past + null = future

People in technology are imaginary, at best, and null once meaningful data has been extracted into value. Things speed up. Technological industrialization was a scientific endeavor, clinical in its approach to expansion and the redefinition of social positions in relation to machines.[18] Previously, Western monarchies enriched their empires through the labor of enslaved people. Kings were replaced with capital cities, or metropolises, where government and economic strength sat and fanned out to areas of production. The metropolis dictated an identity for the state and empire. The pride of being a born citizen was created by the metropolis, and with industrialization, the metropolis created centralized education to normalize a central identity and eliminate difference. This education was designed to transmit the information required to turn people from peasants into citizens and workers who could then populate centers of industrial production.[19] The cultural material of social hierarchies, with slavery at its core, was remediated.

This small shift is the difference between slavery and colonization: in colonization people and places are attached to a government, whereas in slavery they are attached to individuals. This shift then created the archetype for the colonial sentimentality that would enable empathy culture to come into being. And empathy is psychic slavery for the disempowered, marginalized, and oppressed. Empathy is a state of nonmovement through time or space, where the Other is always suffering, even in moments of joy, mediated through whiteness. In moments of panic by people who fear the Other, the slave, the oppressed, or the colonized, attempts are made to grab hold of their own full humanity. This leads to punishment, sacrifice, and murder. When the sacrifice occurs, there is a reflexive call for collective empathy, with a disturbing twist. Every call to empathy for the sacrificed leads to exponentially more calls to empathize with the perpetrators, to understand their motivations, their fear, their reason for wielding their weapons and doling out death. Technologies expedite this process of empathizing and seeing only the fullness of those in power.

Technologies are built within society and culture to sustain the power structures of the past into the future. In popular culture, "neutrality" is used as a euphemism for "unbiased and unfeeling" and for the purpose of negating existing structures of power. Technologies and their inability to feel allow them to uphold power structures indiscriminately. The photographs of Héliani exist side by side with those of war because the photographer who saw so much beauty in the people he encountered was in Africa to film the French military presence. He was a member of the military and, as he said, his camera was loaded and ready to shoot. The portraits of "Hottentot types" carefully posed next to photographs of European types across ethnicities neutralizes the ideological racism we live with today, which is responsible for the invention of the *Hottentot*. Technologies, in addition to containing their own accident, also contain their own perceived neutralization by subsuming everyone equally across time and space.[20] Technologies are two-way mirrors. Technological mirrors reflect the past onto people alive today and allow for the reflection of today into the future. Technology reproduces, sustains, and reduces resistance. Technological tools enable prescriptive engagements in the configuration of

the past-us = the future.

Emerging technologies create the illusion of progress. All technologies, especially emerging ones, arrest movement to ensure that user mobility is limited by the affordances and accessibility built into the tools. Today's emerging technologies impose a false connection through the digital world and assume the inability to connect to certain pasts and places is a neutral act. People today live with the expositional nature of social media and actively curate and erase personae or types. We accept that entering into this practice is difficult for certain people to participate in because of digital divides. People become digital information both consciously through social media and algorithmically through their data trails. In the meantime, users position themselves as spectacle and spectator. Suffering is consumed on a loop through devices that connect across distance, from Syria, to Black people of all ages and genders being killed, to the exploitation and abuse of children, to the continued displacement of Indigenous communities. This is the wrath of colonization, industrialized and technologically efficient. Colonization is built into every technology and new media form. In this world, optimal efficiency is either hoarding all the power and means of reproduction or death. This is exceptionally human, not dystopian. If empathy were a real possibility, it would not fix us.

Artificial ignorance: History and the short-term memory of technology.

The *Journal of Artificial Intelligence* was launched in 1970. The abstract of its first article, "The Correctness of Nondeterministic Programs" by Zohar Manna, states the following:

> In this paper we formalize properties of non-deterministic programs by means of the satisfiability and validity of formulas in first-order logic. Our main purpose is to emphasize the great variety of possible applications of the results, especially for solving problems of the kind: "Find a sequence of actions that will achieve a given goal."[21]

Artificial intelligence assumes the past has the answers to the future's questions. Algorithms, though complex, are still artifacts of what came before. Smart cars use AI to self-drive, theoretically to prevent crashes but in reality also causing them. AI controls the supply chain as goods move around the world (or to people's homes with same-day delivery). Organizations are increasingly interested in how AI can improve internal workflows, processes, and the efficiency of their workers, students, or customers. The autonomous and AI–powered future removes culpability for the accident of existence and the inequality therein; technology allows individuals to claim that they are no longer in control of the interaction and thus somehow not responsible for the aftereffects. Examples already exist from law enforcement, illustrating how this future will maintain uneven power dynamics while still taking advantage of all the privileges of birthright.

The artificial ignorance, then, is the lack of recognition of colonization, oppression, and slavery as conditions through which the current world was made and on which it continues to depend. Artificial ignorance reduces people to representational objects. More often than not, those with the least power face the gravest technologically inscribed oppression. Empathy and progress make this reality appear as though it is an inevitability and, given the circumstances, the best possible version of the world. Progress and empathy cannot become the artificial and theoretical frames with which to explain why some are left behind while others thrive. Fixing the inability to feel suffering and refocusing on the realm of the privileged as the key to understanding what is happening to those "poor Black and Brown people over there" is critical, since digital media makes physically shipping people in and keeping them in enclosures for an artificial encounter at the zoo unnecessary. The digital enclosure is everywhere, and everyone is always a click away.

The field of artificial intelligence reduces humans to input/output machines. Empathy is the affective space of the human reduced to a flat interior experience. With the right combination of technologies and related influences, empathy can transcribe an experience of a person into technological data and then regurgitate it as "meaningful" to other people. Even better, technology can throw out the human altogether, transmit the affective ghost of a person, and place it into the empathetic process of another person, who drops in through technology to imagine the past experience of an Other as their own. As much as Cartesian duality, where mind and matter are separated, is rejected, empathy relies on the thought/experience duality but breaks their connection to each other.

This suggests that it's not just the algorithms that are biased but also the training sets and all the processes that involve people.[22] This means that even if people are brought in from diverse backgrounds to train the algorithm, the choices offered from the start contain the biases of those putting them together. By the time a decision is made to create a mediated experience, either algorithmically or through low-tech media such as the stages of human zoos, the bias is already built in: all from the very first thought of the person who directs or produces the encounter. It is imperative not to ignore the body already conceived and interacted with by the mind, as that body is the body of technological inspiration. The ability to empathize with it or to humanize it makes the technological future.

Decolonial cultural analytics.

Cultural analytics posits that we turn large quantities of images into data sets that can be analyzed outside of their cultural context to find underlying patterns.[23] The aesthetic focus happening in new media studies invites us to look at data in the opposite way when it is brought into conversation with decolonizing projects. When we think of the colonial or enslaved body, the data has already been culturally synthesized into a series of archetypes and social roles. The belief that technically enabled solutions will somehow move us forward ignores a truth embedded in technologies: even when they are critically created and deployed, rather than freeing society from the ills of humanity, they usually speed us toward our demise. The digital world, combined with new and emerging technologies, carries oppression, marginalization, annihilation at the speed of light. Thinking back to the digital image of Héliani surrounded by white men: she embodied, for an instant, all the sexual horrors we place on Black women in the psychic space where we imagine what actual colonization and enslavement were like. The ability of the viewers of the photograph to place Héliani in a cultural context illustrates, for some, that the work of cultural analytics is a forgone conclusion. Calls for more empathy in all these spaces are calls for death.

Empathy's undoing of humanity, especially when technologically mediated, is a dialectic that is a very particular type of undoing predicated on time stopping for some. If the basic contours of Fanon's decolonized dialectic are, per George Ciccariello-Maher, in *Decolonizing Dialectics*, "its attentiveness to nonbeing, the violent project of identity to set frozen history into motion, and radical open-endedness that foregrounds rupture at the expense of closure," then empathy is surely a colonial impulse that attempts to prevent this rupture.[24] What is accomplished by attempting to travel through and at times under the time of the Other, that unreachable someone, somewhere, somewhen? Disconnection renders simultaneity an impossibility, even as it feels like emotional accomplishment and knowing. Fanon states it thus, in *The Wretched of the Earth:*

> Decolonization, which sets out to change the order of the world, is clearly an agenda for total disorder. But it cannot be accomplished by the wave of a magic wand, a natural cataclysm, or a gentleman's agreement. Decolonization, we know, is an historical process: In other words, it can only be understood, it can only find its significance and become self-coherent insofar as we can discern the history-making movement which gives it form and substance. Decolonization is the encounter between two congenitally antagonistic forces that in fact owe their singularity to the kind of reification secreted and nurtured by the colonial situation. Their first confrontation was colored by violence and their cohabitation—or rather the exploitation of the colonized by the colonizer—continued at the point of the bayonet and under cannon fire. The colonist and the colonized are old acquaintances. And consequently, the colonist is right when he says he "knows" them. It is the colonist who fabricated and continues to fabricate the colonized subject. The colonist derives his validity, i.e., his wealth, from the colonial system.[25]

Colonization desires to occupy not just the present but the past and the future. Empathy stops time for Others and temporarily allows the empathizer to metaphorically disappear into the Other's imagined despair. There is no way to balance the suffering of and from the past. The heaviness of the impossibility is what empathy tries to lighten. The drive to internalize the suffering of Others through empathy ensures that the psychic fishhook of colonization is embedded in societies across the globe. Empathy is a colonial affect designed to ensure that some continue to culturally exist only through suffering, while others consume that suffering as an object designed for diversion. Technology allows the suffering to be reproduced en masse.

A decolonial aesthetic project requires latching onto the moments of humanness. Decolonial analytics understands that the colonial matrix of power requires the past to speak or to imagine the Other into being. If there is a need to understand domination/exploitation/conflict, then empathy's spaces of dominion are thought/body/time.[26] The role of guilt and suffering has been converted into a gamified experience in which a person imagines their body one way or steps into an experience that forces their body to exist as if the analog experience were their own. Examining how people are understood through their bodies and the temporal contexts of their lives gives us a better understanding of who we are today. When looking at emerging technology, it is important to ask what version of thought/body/time they freeze by foreclosing other possibilities?

With the current form of media and technology, as driven by data and algorithms, a carceral counterpart of cultural analytics has emerged: predictive analytics.[27] Predictive analytics software claims to take a neutral stance to determine the actions a person is likely to make based on various, often secret data points. Unsurprisingly, this was very exciting for law enforcement, a subject explored in the *ProPublica*'s article "Machine Bias," in 2016.[28] Empathy, in all these new and emerging digital technologies, spurred by electricity, light, and underlying human-created code, bridges cultural analytics and predictive analytics.

Empathy requires a culturally predictive analytical mindset in which it makes sense that a certain person or set of people should suffer, be disempowered, removed from society, or imprisoned. It also requires the subject to believe that these things will never happen to them. Finally, the subject has to believe in the superiority of technology, algorithms, and the current power structure so that those things can come together to create and/or code a consistent and scalable experience as well as a universally accepted response.

The resulting experience creates the correct and just affective response to the existence of the Other, or a predictive response for a potential future encounter. This experience should remind anyone who goes through it that the Other is imprisoned in their "lack," or suffering. But first, the data must be collected.

Deep Empathy AI project.

MIT's Media Lab created a UNICEF innovation project. The project collects donations for UNICEF's Help Syrian Children campaign. Who doesn't love children? Given how disturbing the Deep Empathy project is, I am not sure the creators do. Here is the project description:

> **AI-INDUCED EMPATHY**
>
> *Can we use AI to increase empathy for victims of far-away disasters by making our homes appear similar to the homes of victims?*
>
> **Deep Empathy** gets you closer to the realities of those that suffer the most, by helping you imagine what neighborhoods around the world would look like if hit by disaster.[29]

This project fixes a gaze and assumes that those who suffer are less valuable than the buildings where the potential empathizer might be situated. Technological limitations mean the heat, smells, pain, hunger, desperation, 360-degree sound, shock, and the actual experience of war zones cannot reach the person using AI and allows them instead to imagine a war as though it were their own.

Every new iteration of technology demands the erasure of previous cultural structures to enable an optimized experience. Artificial histories are built onto technological cycles. Empathy AI removes people from their own context and allows them to pretend that a different context belongs to them. Visitors to the site are given the opportunity to train the algorithm. The training portion is one in which a user is served images of people directly impacted, displaced, and killed by this tragedy and asked to **"CLICK ON WHICH IMAGE MAKES YOU FEEL MORE EMPATHETIC TOWARDS VICTIMS OF THE CRISIS IN SYRIA"** (figure 3.2).[30] As an object among machines, "Man is a standardized nonentity among other nonentities: he is confronted by a faceless Machine, efficient, alone, unbelonging, coldly hostile, inherently violent."[31]

Any media used for propaganda are tools of war.[32] This project is war. Anyone who engages with Deep Empathy AI becomes part of an ethically questionable, active battle in line with what all emerging technologies do: ask the visitors to help calibrate some portion of the experience that is not explicitly defined. Thus, visitors are asked to choose who or what is more deserving of death or protection. When the photographs are a person versus a building, the question is, "What is more worthy to remain standing after the inevitable destruction?" The decision has already been made, though. Empathy assumes that people are disposable. The creators of Deep Empathy wrote the program with this knowledge and in line with a worldview that attaches feelings to objects and things people can purchase. The assumption built into the project is that people will care more about their own homes, devoid of people and destroyed, rather than engaging with the totality of the dead, displaced, and suffering. This is war, and war is death:

> Around the world, 50 million children have migrated across borders or been forcibly displaced within their own countries. In Syria alone, the brutal six-year-old war has affected more than 13.5 million people and 80% of the country's children—8.4 million young lives shattered by violence and fear. Hundreds of thousands of people have been displaced and their homes destroyed.
>
> Can you conceptualize these numbers? People generate a response that statistics can't. And technologists—through tools like AI—have opportunities to help people see things differently.
>
> Deep Empathy utilizes deep learning to learn the characteristics of Syrian neighborhoods affected by conflict, and then simulates how cities around the world would look in the midst of a similar conflict. Can this approach—familiar in a range of artistic applications—help us to see recognizable elements of our lives through the lens of those experiencing vastly different circumstances, theoretically a world away? And by helping an AI learn empathy, can this AI teach us to care?[33]

I've gone through and trained the algorithm a few times, never sure what horror I will see. I've seen people aiming guns at people in the photos. Missiles dropping from the sky next to destroyed buildings. Children playing next to images of graves. The most traumatic was, after a series of landscapes, a vividly colored dead and bloodied child being covered in a shroud by a gloved hand, next to a black-and-white picture of a hill somewhere. There

Progress: 38/50

WE COLLECTED TOP IMAGES FOR 'SYRIA WAR' QUERY ON FLICKR AND NEED YOUR HELP TO TEACH AI LEARN EMPATHY! CLICK ON WHICH IMAGE MAKES YOU FEEL MORE EMPATHETIC TOWARDS VICTIMS OF THE CRISIS IN SYRIA.

Fig 3.2. Screenshot from "Deep Empathy," Teach AI training survery, part of a joint project of the MIT Media Lab's Scalable Cooperation and UNICEF Innovation. Last accessed on November 6 2022, deepempathy.mit.edu/survey.

was no context provided. I am simply told, in bold and all caps "**CLICK ON WHICH IMAGE MAKES YOU FEEL MORE EMPATHETIC TOWARDS VICTIMS OF THE CRISIS IN SYRIA**" (see figure 3.2) each time a new photo loads. Because the images are automatically pulled in from a "Syria War" query on Flickr, the creators of Deep Empathy are absolved of culpability for what is shared. Disconnection and destruction. How odd is it, too, that after going through this process, the shortest message is given to the user, along with an invitation to share, is "Congratulations! You've helped teach an AI empathy :)" (figures 3.3 and 3.4).

Given the size of Marshall McLuhan's oeuvre, which includes experimental records, art and experimental books, card games, magazine interviews, and film appearances, as well as traditional books and articles, there are many B-sides to his work that offer correctives to some of his utopian dreams for the electric age.[34] The short McLuhan essay "The New Art or Science Which the Electronic or Post-Mechanical Age Has to Invent Concerns the Alchemy of Social Change" is one of those texts.[35] It starts with the damning statement, "We can no longer tolerate the irresponsibility of social trial and error. When information moves instantly to all parts of the

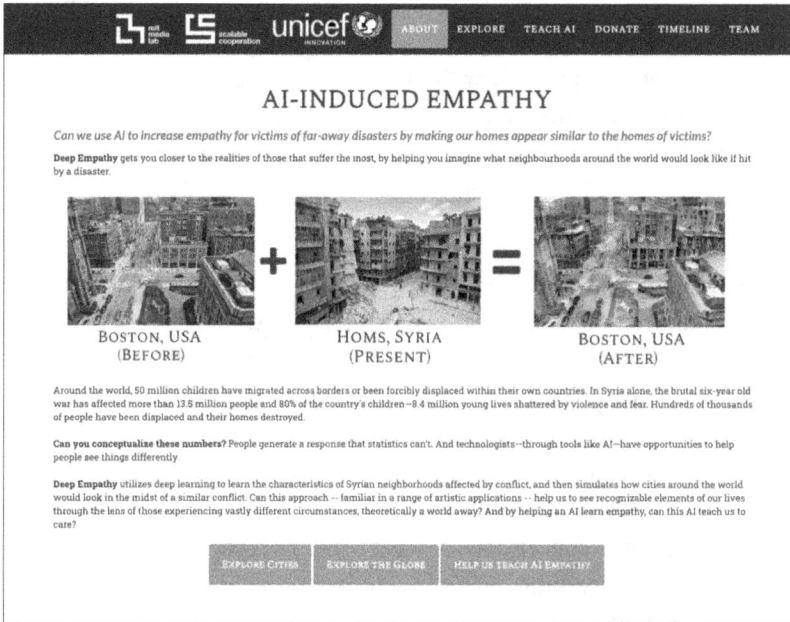

Fig 3.3. Screenshot from the "Deep Empathy" home page, part of a joint project of the MIT Media Lab's Scalable Cooperation, and UNICEF Innovation, accessed on November 6, 2022, deepempathy.mit.edu.

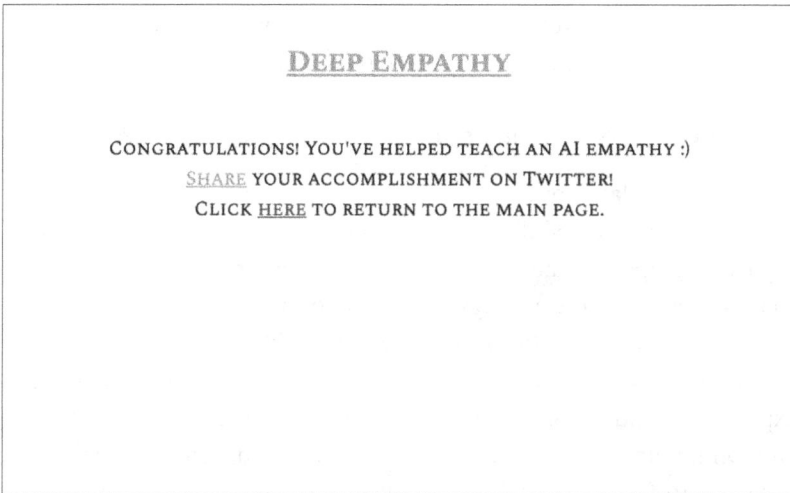

Fig 3.4. "Becoming Homeless," VR experience eviction notice. From "Becoming Homeless: A Human Experience," Virtual Human Interaction Lab, Stanford University, 2020, accessed on December 2, 2018, http://vhil.stanford.edu/becoming homeless/.

globe it is chemically explosive. Any chain-reaction which occurs rapidly is explosive, whether in personal or social life." Empathy is social trial and error. Deep Empathy attempts to algorithmically scale and speed up this social trial and error through a programmed journey into the world in which people already exist. To feel for the Other requires imagining one's own death and annihilation. McLuhan, again:

> It is the normal aspect of our information-flow which is revolutionary now. The new media normalize the state of revolution which is war. Two hundred years ago it was idea and theory which disrupted the old regimes. Now it is just the package information which we call entertainment which transforms living conditions and basic attitudes. It is the ordinary flow of news and pictures from every quarter of the globe which rearranges our intellectual and emotional lives without either struggle or acceptance on our part.
>
> Our present conceptions of what constitutes social cause and effect and influence are quite unable to cope with this electronic simultaneity of conspicuous co-existence. . . .
>
> The same technology which has made instantaneous information-flow a chemical danger to every culture in the world has also created the power of total re-construction and pre-construction of models of situations. . . . Instead of a *view* of the past we simply re-create a model of it. . . .
>
> When all kinds of information flowed slowly in a society, educational irrelevance could be corrected by self-education and by individual brilliance.
>
> **THAT WON'T WORK TODAY**[36]

Technology today moves information at the speed of light and creates experiences with the ability to cause damage as big as any other type of explosive. Empathy is not a salve to the speed or damage of today's digital technologies. The larger ecology of information-flows from war-torn countries such as Syria transforms what was once editorialized coverage from people on the ground or with subject expertise into a sterile automated experience without context. The project dismantles the flow of information and communication; as a result, people are impacted through visualizing a false reality of destruction. The unspoken message is that people will learn to feel through AI from the (biased) views of those who spend time training the Deep Empathy algorithm. It is an attempt to force a slow-down and make it effective for a world in which information-flows are overwhelming and move quickly. The project is biased because of those who either truly believe they can calibrate the algorithm through pictorial comparison or those who, tongue-in-cheek, go in to feel the suffering of others and find joy or glee in that suffering.

Technically feeling.

Bikolabs, an intervention studio of Biko, a Spanish design firm with offices in Madrid, Pamplona, and Lima, released an English-language digital creative project called "Empathizing with AI's Psyche."[37] The project argues that we humans have not been treating AI fairly and need to work on feeling empathetic toward AI. It starts with the following text:

EMPATHIZING WITH AI'S PSYCHE

We have to admit it.

We have been harsh to image recognition articificial [*sic*] intelligence.

We have mercilessly forced them to perform complex tasks and mocked them thereafter due to unexpected results.

However, this situation has to change. It's about time for **a massive empathetic exercise** toward AI to take place. We have to start understanding at once how they "see" everyday objects.

It is imperative to empathize with them right away. In the near future, AI will perform particular tasks such as agriculture and cattle raising monitoring, medical diagnosis, big data tagging, or autonomous weapons guiding.

Yet ourselves, human beings, behaving like sociopaths we have assigned to AI, intricate tasks like detecting a tipped over fire truck, telling the difference between a Husky and wolf in the snow, recognizing a drill carried by a woman, or even distinguishing between a pan and a wok.[38]

The website shows an animated image of the objects in the last sentence. Immediately after the image, it states, "Definitely, it has not been a fair treatment! / Therefore, we should connect ourselves to their nervous system and glimpse the machine's psyche!"[39] After this, there is a brief explanation of how AI works, and then, much like Deep Empathy AI, there is a training set. Rather than seeing images of people and war, the user is asked to view blurred images and that are preassigned to a category and guess what the images are. The level of image blur is determined by how accurate AI systems are, on average.

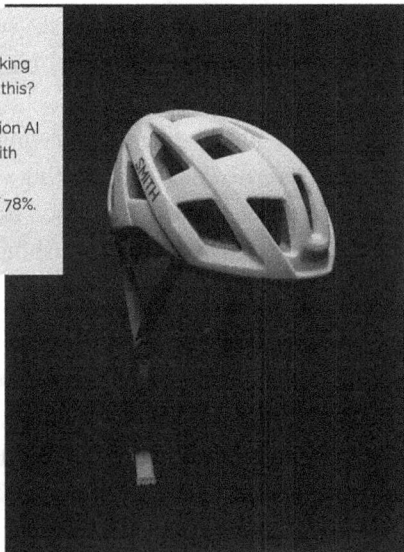

Figs 3.5–3.7.

This mimics how an AI might see an object, followed by a reveal of the object, which is usually not related to the category/identification the AI assigned to it; but the object is then put into context and shown in an array of images from the *category* to which the AI assigned it. Going through the process allows an individual to see, technically, the way an AI might *see* (it cannot be asked to verify the accuracy of the experience), while at the same time apprehending how limited AI vision is. The question I am left with from the experience, though, is: "Is this really *empathizing* with the AI?" My inability to guess left me humored and frustrated at the same time. I do not think AI has actual emotional responses to its failures, nor does it have the capacity to realize that the algorithm programming has failed.

Unlike the violence of creating new worlds, the violence of technologically mediated empathy is colonial in that it asks people to feel for technology and its processes while disregarding the distributed remnants of people who travel across time and space as digital information. Technology and digital media turn the body into the ultimate factory. It is beyond being the product that is sold to advertisers; it's more like a belief that there is something inside the Other that is attainable, and not proprietary or meaningful unless mined, reproduced, and commodified. The empathetic impulse is the ultimate expression of this. It is when we look to Others and their experiences to create our own humanity.

Digital technologies and emerging media, with their lack of movement, fungibility, and stability in terms of their content, are designed for a certain affective response. This response is often steeped in the colonial imaginary and provides only glimpses of blurred images and categories, leaving the individual user to fill in the missing information. Bodies and human experience become a reproductive tool with which to always achieve the right emotional outcome for those in power or for those imagined as the "neutral" human figure. We speak as though we are reacting to an artifact. I wrote about photos, but in reality, it was the people who made me feel something; or rather, it was the collage of my imagination and the glimpses in the archive that turned the photos into people for me. Technology leaves limited space to question how literate we are in reading lives and bodies as we reduce them to archive objects with which to generate feelings.[40]

Empathy is an ontological relationship toward the Other. Empathy is portrayed as universally good, but this judgment has been made without critical inquiry into its mechanics or ethics and without inquiry into the harms it perpetrates in its approach to understanding the Other. As empathy becomes embedded in emerging media and technology, understanding the work that empathy does is imperative. It is deeply colonial and about the self as settler. The desire to occupy the Other to the point of not needing the Other to be there, as is the case with so many modern technologies, erases the need for the Other altogether. This is colonization at its ultimate efficiency. The Other and the land of the Other need not exist, because both have been moved completely to psychic space, eliminating the need for fertile land and people all together.

What happens if we approach empathy as a constructed experience, a tool, or a technology deployed to put cultural analytics to work on marginalized bodies? Empathy makes the human component of an individual extractable, transferable, and reproducible by anchoring itself in actual bodies and lived experiences. The person, othered and excluded from society, is left to prove their worth and value by demonstrating that their suffering can help those more privileged believe that they understand the suffering of the Other, all without having to taint their sacred bodies with firsthand experience of suffering.

The affective construction erases or relegates the person or people suffering to the background. Their experiences remain, locked in time, and "endanger man by rendering man himself a standing reserve."[41] There is a bit more than a standing reserve when looking at empathy, though. Rather than hunting for future potential, empathy mines a person for their memories and encodes their perceived or imagined affective responses, transferring memoires that then become those of the empathizer. The body remains as archive, and the marginalized person experiences a metaphorical death. The companies and people who own the platforms that allow for the exchange of the digital artifact, per Tonia Sutherland, "those who benefit from systemic and structural racism are, quite literally, 'making a killing' by inscribing and reinscribing death and trauma and befitting socially, culturally, politically, and economically."[42]

Twinning.

Even more than an ideology, empathy follows things being established in digitally augmented manufacturing. Manufacturing has a concept called the "digital twin." In a 2018 interview, Jason Shepherd, Chief Technology Office of Internet of Things and Edge Computing at Dell Technologies, described it as such:

> a notion of a digital representation like a full embodiment of a physical form ... the real part of a digital twin is that you're using sensor-based data to put back into that model what's performed and how it's performing in the actual world. . . . So it's both the physical form, and the dynamics of that coordinated real time based on sensing that's pulling data out of the physical world and putting it back into its twin in the digital world.[43]

Though the concept of the digital twin is used primarily in the realm of disaster prevention or technology optimization to run computer simu-lated models that are constantly fed real-world inputs, it can be applied to emerging technologies and social media. Even before the announcement of the partnerships between Meta and ten universities to create "digital twin" Metaversities, there were Meta VR headsets that came with cameras on the headset and required lights be on so the camera could see.[44] The Oculus app that users downloaded to their phones or tablets requested access to location information, contacts, files, and media. Additionally, the headset had to be attached to a real and active Facebook account. The digital twin for Meta users was not the digital version of their various experiences. The data profile Meta had through the use across their services of social media, photo sharing, messaging, and VR created a digital twin in real time. The digital twin allowed the actions and desires of the end user to be modeled and manipulated by content served in the future. The future content, previously approved by the virtual twin, dictated action in the actual, or nondigital, world.

This prescriptive aspect of technologies and technological modes of communication insinuates connection and understanding. The connection and understanding being "more real" than reality is the gimmick being sold by companies like Meta. In reality, these technologies create distance. Empathy becomes the cure to overcome the distance. If an end user is unable to connect and affectively be the Other, the problem is that person, not the tool. Technologically mediated encounters allow users to feel as the Other. This is modern technological determinism and destruction. The Other of the affection does not exist anymore. Empathy puts immediacy on pause to allow for emotional buffering, transmission, and translation of the digital twin.

Going back to the Metaversities' digital twin project, this reads like an attempt to whitewash the fact that they have a captive audience with clear predictors of success, such as grades and course feedback, to show whether the tests that will be running in the background are successful. This is represented in the press releases with statements such as, "Last year, accountancy firm PwC published research on the advantages of using VR for learning. The findings showed that 40% of VR learners are more confident in applying what they've been taught and 150% more engaged. In addition, VR was found to be 400% faster than classroom-based learning."[45] The initial seven of the ten schools that were announced have an enrollment of more than 165,000 students. That is a potential target test group that, if they are enrolled in a course that is using their digital twin campus features, has to log on to learn. Though it may *feel* similar to Second Life, the avatar-based digital world that previously occupied a similar space in the imaginary of superusers that VR is playing today, the digital twin language hides what is likely really happening or else other language without meaning would likely have been used. Rather than the avatar and experience of the student being defined in real time in a predefined world as is the case with Second Life, in the Metaversity, the world will be constantly evolving, as will the student's digital twin, based on the real-world inputs: always a step ahead in a way that will be invisible to the student. Whereas the student thinks that the course is in real time, a layer of it will be coercing the student's experiences and emotional responses into being at the speed of a supercomputer.

The metaverse, with its drive to make the virtual as close to the real as possible, going so far as to link to things that will feed real-time data to the virtual world, is exactly the work of the digital twin. In manufacturing the digital twin is tied to optimization, profit, preventive and predictive maintenance models, life cycle management, end of service, and shop floors. It has long been known that people are the product of these digital platforms. That the digital twin model is now in this space explicitly highlights that what is happening industrially should be paid attention to, both so we know what is next in terms of technology's need to construct and extract our feelings for profit and so we make sure we do not lose sight of which version of ourselves is real.

Ideologies are reproduced across all forms of cultural production. In the technological society, technologies tell us who we are collectively. The digital twin provides us with an opportunity to think through empathy itself as a cognitive technology of mediation. With empathy, the call is for the person to go into their own head and imagine themselves as Other, a twin. With this twin that exists in the realm of imagination, the individual takes the twin through the experience of becoming the Other. Based on the reaction of that twin to the data input from the Other, the actual self can then claim to know or understand better and, as the myth goes, will subsequently engage in different behavior. This brings us back to the empathetic gaze. The desire to end guilt is achieved because the twin takes on suffering in place of the person, absolving the actual person of guilt. The physical form, then, follows a predetermined path based on the data; the configuring data—the data for care, feeling, and affect—now has this new imagined realm of experience that is used for the individual to assume a more elevated position.

Technology assumes a beginning, a middle, and an end. There is an assumption that empathy leads to action in a technology that is already deployed. Empathy is often positioned as the human solution to the technologically mediated biases of society. For all the work we do to engage critically with technology, especially as it begins to intersect with the margins and borders of society, empathy is brought in without an engagement with what it is and what it is not. Empathy is assumed to be neutral in society, as is technology. However, empathy is able to hide from critical engagement, because no one can truly know the mind of the Other. If technology needs to exist on an affective plane, why must it be the plane of the Other, and not my own? If I start with my own affective plane, I can question why I feel the way I do, and dig deeper into what it means for me, from my positionality, to exist and feel in the technological society.

There is a collective avoidance or fear of dehumanizing the self virtually, as though that dehumanization will manifest itself into reality. It becomes easier to feel into the not-fully-human Other, so that my humanity may be inserted into an experience perceived as incomplete, because I am not a part of it. We do this to avoid the reality that we are all already dehumanized by capital and capitalistic technology. The socially constructed empathy solution, then, with its predefined other side, functions like technology to uphold the belief that it is only the few who require the extra work to be humanized. After all, I've been asked to survive Ebola and become homeless through the titular "empathy machine," but any time I get to pretend to be rich and powerful I am just playing a game.[46]

Technological empathy through connection and understanding signifies technological benevolence. Technological empathy follows the following laws of media:

a. Technological empathy enhances the distance from the Other.
b. Technological empathy obsolesces, pushes aside, or displaces the Other.
c. The lack of need for the Other to exist obsolesces the need of the Other for the experience to be real or to matter; the Other is technologically created or designed to just be an imaginative internalization.
d. Technological empathy does not require the Other to exist.
e. Technological empathy annihilates the existence of the Other because there is only the self while asking for self-annihilation because the self becomes Other.
f. Technological empathy limits understanding by distancing the Other from their own experience, and increasing dissociation of the empathizer by digital twin optimization instead of from experiences in the actual world.[47]

Or, more simply, technological empathy produces enlightened apathy.

Some end thoughts.

If I didn't define myself for myself, I would be crunched into other people's fantasies for me and eaten alive.
—Audre Lorde, "Learning from the 60s"

Change in kind.

"But Jade, what makes any of this different from a novel?" is a common question I hear. It is something that has always made me uncomfortable. We choose to read novels and connect or not connect with the characters they contain. It is okay to dislike a novel or to say, "This genre isn't for me." And while yes, one may feel for or identify with a character in a novel, that character is not an actual person, alive or dead. It is known that they are imaginary. The novel is not approached as though it were reality with real-life consequences for the characters in the book and their descendants (who may never be written into existence).

Empathy is about imagining real people. In that way, perhaps what people are conveying to me is that when they empathize with people, those people are as real to them as the characters in novels. Ancestors reduced to their oppression undergo a change in kind. Rather than being individuals, they become symbols and remnants of oppression across time. This is a psychic death. Unlike characters in a novel, their lives and its stories are not easily bookended. They were, and so we are. Empathy, as it is manifested through the imagined suffering of the Other, is not about recognizing trauma; it is about creating human-made crisis over and over again. Traumatic events end. Empathy binds to some past suffering, disallowing any departure toward the future. Each new encounter with past suffering is a psychic bookend. To participate in modern society and culture without technological aids or to not leave digital traces are impossible. There is no universal altruistic savior who will swoop in and neutralize the trauma inflicted across generations. There is no keyword or concept that will unite everyone other than acknowledging that all humans are human.

Engaging in conversations about empathy illuminates two concepts that are more precise than "empathy." They are "understanding" and "acceptance." There is a drive to understand and accept affective resonance with others. It is, at times, an impossibility that needs to be accounted for so that others are permitted to exist as fully realized people. Seeing one's own house reduced to rubble does not give one some primordial understanding of what it means to live in a war zone. Walking with someone as they pray because they survived a pandemic does not give one access to the trauma and guilt of surviving.

Even when the end of a story is known because there is enough distance between it and now, as with Héilani, it is impossible to piece together so many aspects of the other person's experience. Acceptance in these instances stays in the realm of speculation. And then there are Lisbeth and Jacob, making sense of the world and trying to enact agency and resistance, even as the understanding we apply to their stories is steeped in exploitation and spectacle. Lisbeth's resistance and Jacob's hedonistic desires are lost to the void. We focus on the structure of the human zoo, colonization, and other remnants of colonial power. Our need to focus on these things and not on the people is further evidence of the colonization of psychic space. This is the realm just outside of memory and the shared history of colonial domination. Technologies continue to assert that the experience of the self is about empathy for the Other.

When examining the relationship today has with the past, any interrogation of the past today cannot be with the real past. It is a reflexive act of world-making that will, by design, contain both the ideologies of the past and of today. By acknowledging where the "I" is looking, how it is seeing, and what its aims are, there is an expansion of acceptance that can lead to new understandings without the need to empathize. Today the digital world is ground zero for acceptance, as is evidenced by the uncritical belief in connection and empathy that comes from innovators in these fields. These innovators are desperately trying to order society around themselves and outsource the ability to feel for others to inhuman, algorithmic, self-driving technologies. The turn toward empathy reaffirms the social and cultural order of the past and does not allow a radical reimagining of the present and the future. There are no longer human zoos in major cities across the world, because human zoos and ethnological shows are now part of the global cultural fabric. Even without a physical barrier and enclosure, people who are different remain spectacles. This is the ideology of empathy.

Empathy itself is an ideology.[1] As Gramsci said, "It is asserted that a given political solution is 'ideological'—i.e., that it is not sufficient to change the structure, although it thinks that it can do so."[2] Because empathy is used as a tool to assuage guilt when concern isn't possible, it does not help those who are suffering. Empathy maintains the supremacy of those with power. It makes morality a project of the individual and, in doing so, makes the suffering of those on the margins a necessity—so that the structures that created such suffering remain unquestioned, continually reproduced through new forms of technology and mediation. The class that has the means of material production at its disposal, consequently, also controls the means of mental production, so that the ideas of those who lack the means of mental production are subject to it.[3]

The past created a technological society instead of a human society with technology. This framework ensures an intense reification of the existing social orders based on a belief that only a few select groups can be recognized as fully human. It inscribes a false truth and belief system across society. Per Clair W. Huntington Jr. and Namgyal Wangchen, "Conventional truth is the means, the truth of the highest meaning is the goal, and one who does not appreciate the distinction between these two treads the wrong path through his reified concepts."[4] Processing thought/body/time through empathy is imagining the Other into being, but not as they are. The impossibility of a self-production coexisting with production from another is an impossibility that runs throughout *Black Skins, White Masks*. From the first line ("The explosion will not happen today. It is too soon ... or too late"), to the breaking into little pieces, to the footnote on Lacan and the broken mirror phase, to the train encounter:

> I came into the world imbued with the will to find a meaning in things, my spirit filled with the desire to attain to the source of the world, and then I found that I was an object in the midst of other objects.

Sealed into that crushing objecthood, I turned beseechingly to others. Their attention was a liberation, running over my body suddenly abraded into nonbeing, endowing me once more with an agility that I had thought lost, and by taking me out of the world, restoring me to it. But just as I reached the other side, I stumbled, and the movements, the attitudes, the glances of the other fixed me there, in the sense in which a chemical solution is fixed by a dye. I was indignant; I demanded an explanation. Nothing happened. I burst apart. Now the fragments have been put together again by another self.[5]

Violent and unconditional love that has emptied out the self must let go of empathy because it is always both too early and too late. We face ourselves despite oppression and suffering. We recognize that to decolonize is to allow the unimagined, the better, the "yes" to manifest so we can move forward to somewhen together. To decolonize empathy, we must strive to create a world full of new and unimagined potentials that enable coexistence. We must recognize the universals and particulars of the oppression and suffering that are just as much a part of human experience as joy and love. As Charif Quellel states in "Frantz Fanon and Colonized Man":

> Therefore to Fanon, Revolution meant, in the final analysis, regeneration. It reasserts the membership of the colonized man, of the damned of the earth, within the human family by providing a method whereby that membership can be realized. Beyond his conflicts and excesses, his loyalties and enmities, his hate and love, beyond the simplistic formulations of both his disciples and critics, Fanon was a man who attempted and succeeded in setting an example of lucidity, courage, and compassion. He accepted the challenge of revolutionary commitment, but without succumbing to either smugness or self-righteousness. He acted without betraying that "something which he had seen before his death," not simply the mystery of violence, but the brotherhood of man.[6]

Each person creates their own ghosts: "What became, was lied, and is finished sinks back into the stream of the past. We leave it behind us when we step into new experiences; it loses its primordiality but remains the 'same experience.' First it is alive and then dead, but not first non-psychic and then psychic."[7] This is the power and the downfall of empathy, because we are not beings who have given in to transcendental consciousness. Empathy is shaped by culture and technology in a never-ending cycle of recreating oppression and its theories without language or its theories aimed at its destruction. The only refuge is within the self, a place where our independent hauntings allow the other side to be more-or-less real. Today is the other side of the past. Empathy limits the past to the future's feelings about it and ensures that some people are only understood as suffering.

Toward an active other and other ways of being.

Suffering is part of the transcendental as it is central to the human condition. Rather than that being a reason to internalize and intellectualize the suffering of the Other, it is rather a call to see and acknowledge it, to listen and to accept it. The recreation of suffering that empathy demands is not moving forward. It is constantly looking back and putting the sufferer in stasis. Mutual recognition requires letting go of some level of control/power and agency.[8] It assumes an active Other, equally engaged and valued in the process of meaning-making. Mutual recognition is accepting without understanding, and it is believing that this acceptance of the value of another is reciprocated. Mutual recognition is not about cognizing the Other into being. It is recognizing that the Otherness is mutual. To decolonize something as pervasive as empathy is to understand that the power of colonization resides in how it imprisons the oppressor who attempts to empathize while continuing the cycle of oppression. The cycle is created each time empathy is extended to people who are only worthy of existence through empathy.

Five things that get in the way of mutual recognition are as follows:

1. Power
2. Reciprocity
3. Fear
4. Status Quo
5. Cognition

Empathy does not automatically lead to failure of these things, but it is annihilation. If, for books, we are comfortable saying the author is dead, through empathy, we are comfortable with the Other being dead, too.

Notes.

By way of an introduction.

1 Lipps, "Einfühlung, innere Nachahmung und Organenempfindungen"; Stein, *On the Problem of Empathy*; Bloom, *Against Empathy*.

2 Hume, *A Treatise of Human Nature*, 365.

3 Hume, *A Treatise of Human Nature*, 363.

4 This is in "Book II. Of the Passions" in Hume, *A Treatise of Human Nature*. The interesting thing about the section of this book is that the quotes most often used are related to possessing objects, giving possessions, and the pleasure that derives from these acts. I think it is important to note that the emotions discussed were positive emotions and sentiments in this instance, whereas empathy is used in the context of negative emotions or experiences.

5 Matravers, "Empathy and the Danger of Inventing Words."

6 Hogan, "Development of an Empathy Scale," 308.

7 Matravers, "Empathy and the Danger of Inventing Words."

8 Batson, "These Things Called Empathy," 3.

9 Batson, "These Things Called Empathy," 9.

10 *Third world* here refers to the original French meaning of *tiers monde*, which implied the country was part of a Communist bloc.

11 The television series was broken up into seven "universal" life stages, "Married Life," "Children," "Teenagers," "Weddings," "Birth," "Old Age," and "Death."

12 Pedwell, "Theorizing 'African' Female Genital Cutting and 'Western' Body Modifications," 64.

13 Guilt here is understood through the developmental lens established by Winnicott. I am also influenced by the idea of "transformative guilt," a subject often talked about by Martha Crawford on twitter @shrinkthinks. I find these frames productive as they see guilt as a normal and, at times, necessary state of being that isn't just negative. Martha is the one who suggested I read Winnicott.

14 Nakamura, Lisa. 2019. "Virtual Reality and the Feeling of Virtue," 3–3.

15 "6 × 9: A virtual experience of solitary confinement," *Guardian*, accessed September 23, 2022, https://www.theguardian.com/world/ng-interactive /2016/apr/27/6x9-a-virtual-experience-of-solitary-confinement. I want to highlight *The Guardian* project because its creators worked to go beyond the experience by providing articles, resources, podcasts, and other media that delve deeper into solitary confinement from various perspectives. Many VR experiences designed to introduce people to the suffering of others do not provide such supporting materials, and it is worth highlighting ways to address some of the limits of the medium.

16 I often wonder if part of the reason that sharing buttons is so useful on these types of digital experiences is because sharing creates a tiny action that feels like "at least I did something" and alleviates some of the pressure to do something because something, though small and more likely than not inconsequential, was done.

17 Ahmed, *Cultural Politics of Emotion*, 2.

18 Ahmed, *Cultural Politics of Emotion*, 3.

19 Truscott, "Empathy's Echo," 14.

20 McKittrick, "Mathematics Black Life," 16.

21 McKittrick, "Mathematics Black Life" 22.

22 Fanon, *Black Skin, White Masks*, xvi.

23 Truscott, "Empathy's Echo," 15.

24 Oliver, *The Colonization of Psychic Space*, xix.

25 This is a derogatory term. However, without use of the term the work of this book would not be possible due to metadata standards and the "hiddenness" of some of the items explored in this book. In this context, even though the items exist, they are hidden because of the limited data associated with the objects which makes finding the objects more difficult than one that has extensive metadata attached to it.

Chapter 1: The other side of human zoos?

1 Blanchard, Boetsch, and Snoep, *Human Zoos*; Thode-Arora, *From Samoa with Love?*

2 Blanchard, Boetsch, and Snoep, *Human Zoos*, 13.

3   Blanchard, Boetsch, and Snoep, *Human Zoos*, 13.

4   Thode-Arora, *From Samoa with Love?*, 12.

5   *Talofa* is the Samoan equivalent of the Hawaiian word *aloha*.

6   Thode-Arora, *From Samoa with Love?*, 14–15.

7   Sekula, "The Traffic in Photographs."

8   Balme, *Pacific Performances*, 17.

9   Banania is a chocolate cereal drink produced by Unilever. The face of the product features a smiling Senegalese man wearing a fez. The brand is still in existence today. In discussing the role of this advertisement in the French version of *Black Skin, White Masks*, Fanon says that this imagery creates a type that is reproduced across media, from illustrations for children to films. Rather than featuring a realistic drawing of a Senegalese man, it now features a cartoon drawing of a younger looking Senegalese man in a fez with a comically large very toothy smile.

10   Sandau, "Why There Are Tattoos and Strapless Costumes."

11   Hartshorn, "Mormon Education in the Bold Years," 203–5.

12   This quote is from the Polynesian Cultural Center website (https://www .polynesia.com). I've always found it fascinating that we easily talk of "Polynesia," but that is not a real place. It is an idea and, as such, a center like the Polynesian Cultural Center can digitally occupy "polynesia.com."

13   Thode-Arora, *From Samoa with Love?*, 121.

14   The French title of *The Wretched of the Earth* is *Les damnés de la terre*, which can be translated as *the Damned of the Earth*, linking the book to the "veritable hell" in *Black Skins, White Masks*.

15   Innis, *The Bias of Communication*, 75.

16   Coles, *The Uninvited Guest from the Unremembered Past*, xiv.

17   Wallis, "Black Bodies, White Science," 57.

18   Caswell and Cifor, "From Human Rights to Feminist Ethics," 25.

19   Hagenbeck, *Beasts and Men*, 292.

20   Caswell and Cifor, "From Human Rights to Feminist Ethics," 30; 33.

21   Hagenbeck, *Beasts and Men*, 19.

22   Hagenbeck, *Beasts and Men*, 31.

23   Ulrikab, *The Diary of Abraham Ulrikab*.

24   Ulrikab, *The Diary of Abraham Ulrikab*, xviii.

25   Hagenbeck was a world-renowned exotic animal trader and trainer.

26   Hagenbeck, *Beasts and Men*, 16–17.

27   *Sociological Images* is part of the *Society Pages*, which is an open-access project based at the University of Minnesota in the Department of Sociology (https://thesocietypages.org/socimages/). *Sociological Images* describes itself as follows: "Sociological Images is designed to encourage all kinds of people to exercise and develop their sociological imagination by presenting brief sociological discussions of compelling and timely imagery that spans

the breadth of sociological inquiry." That is, they are attempting to bring sociology to the masses. The work, though, especially since imagination and visual culture play a significant role, is prone to cultural biases. When a picture is worth a thousand words, it is important to ask from whom the words are coming, and to what end? See Wade, "Human Zoos at the Turn of the 20th Century."

28 I've put "ally" and "fetishist" together as they both aspire to a seemingly positive relationship to the Other that requires always only seeing the Other as separate from the self and engaging with them from that standpoint. In both instances, the mutuality of the relationship is bound by a personal or social aspect of the Other.

29 Truscott, "Empathy's Echo," 2.

30 Trézenem and Lembezat, *La France équatoriale*; Lembezat, *Kirdi, Mukulehe, Eve Noire. La colonne.*

31 Lembezat, *La colonne, ou, Journal d'un mercenaire hétéroclite.*

32 Translated from the June 1962 issue of *Études: Revue fondée en 1856 par des Pères de la Compagnie de Jésus.* The original can be found at https://gallica .bnf.fr/ark:/12148/bpt6k441763d.

33 Fanon, "The North African Syndrome," 16.

Chapter 2: We have names.

1 Willis and Williams, *The Black Female Body.*

2 Hurston, "How It Feels to Be Colored Me." While this piece is perhaps one of the most well known, it too has its own colonial baggage as it was originally printed in the white Christian periodical *Tomorrow's World.* This reinforces that there is not an outside to this dynamic and that the work is to figure out how to create cracks and lines of flight, which "How It Feels to Be Colored Me" has done successfully.

3 Davoine and Gaudillière, *History beyond Trauma*, 28–29.

4 Fanon, *Black Skins, White Masks*, 1.

5 Campt, *Listening to Images.*

6 Fanon, *Toward the African Revolution*, 14.

7 Lembezat and Carmet, *Eve Noire*, 65–66.

8 Lembezat and Carmet, *Eve Noire*, 66.

9 Lembezat and Carmet, *Eve Noire*, 66.

10 Berger, "From *Ways of Seeing*," 50.

11 Lembezat, *Eve Noire*, 66.

12 The name of the teenage girl, Héliani/Hellani, that this section focuses on is spelled in multiple ways across references. I have included the two most common spellings in the section title to highlight some of the difficulty in finding information across archives and resources.

13 Lefebvre, *Avec de Gaulle en Afrique*, 138.

14   Lefebvre, *Avec de Gaulle en Afrique*, 138.

15   Fanon, *Toward the African Revolution*, 43.

16   The term *Hottentot* is a derogatory term about a made-up group. Today the preferred term is *Khoikhoi*; however, the archives and popular culture still tag material related to this group *Hottentot*. One of the difficulties in doing work on this subject, and the continued circulation of related materials is how to reconcile the used language with what we know today.

17   "Airs Hottentots," a song that was written to accompany the Sunday performances, had sheet music published in *Le Figaro* on September 12, 1888, p. 8 (https://gallica.bnf.fr/ark:/12148/bpt6k2805153). The song is immensely simple, with a deep repetitive chord throughout. I had someone make a recording of it for me. It is so simple. This led me down a digital hole. I spent hours listening to songs and watching videos tagged as "Hottentot" or "Khoisan" traditional songs on YouTube and Archive.org. The collective sound of voices and click consonants, beads banging against each other as they shake, and plucked stringed instruments layered together to create a rich soundscape that is as much about the sound as it is about the movement of the body. None of the songs sounded like "Airs Hottentots."

18   The arrival of the people from South Africa was discussed in a variety of places, including the *Revue d'Anthropologie* (https://gallica.bnf.fr/ark:/12148 /bpt6k442571n) and the *Bulletin de la Société Nationale d'Acclimatation de France* (https://gallica.bnf.fr/ark:/12148/bpt6k54549792). Many of these sources are available through https://gallica.bnf.fr.

19   Ahmed, "The Cultural Politics of Emotion," 33.

20   I added a strikethrough to this text as a way to reject the reading and purpose of it while also acknowledging that the text helps contextualize and give voice to the troupe of people from South Africa who came to Paris.

21   Le Roux, "La vie à Paris," my translation. The original French account is itself an interpretation, because Lisbeth conducted the interview in English.

22   Le Roux, "La vie à Paris."

23   Le Roux, "La vie à Paris."

24   *Le Voleur Illustré*, 491.

25   Breittmayer, "Rapport sur Congrès de Bourg," 127.

26   Topinard, "La stéatopygie des Hottentotes du Jardin d'acclimatation," 194.

27   Delmare, "Chez les Hottentots," my translation. There is no indication of the original language of the interview.

28   Delmare, "Les Hottentots à Paris."

29   Fanon, *Black Skin, White Masks*, 89.

30   Stein, *On the Problem of Empathy*, 69.

31   "Stage Gossip," *New York Herald, European Edition*, September 15, 1888, https://gallica.bnf.fr/ark:/12148/bpt6k4774661d/f1.vertical#.

32   "Direction for Women Smokers: Rules for Their Guidance Prepared by a Parisian Expert," *Chicago Tribune*, October 19, 1888.

33 The writing on his portrait photograph (figure 2.13) reads says Jacobus Much (the image with writing can be viewed at "Hottentots du Jardin d'Acclimatation en 1888, par Fernand Delisle," https://gallica.bnf.fr/ark: /12148/btv1b77021135, images 1 and 2); however, the name is found in other archives (such as Getty's Open Content) is Huch.

34 Hartman, *Wayward Lives, Beautiful Experiments*, xv.

Chapter 3: New media and emerging technology will kill us all, though.

1 Benjamin, "Catching Our Breath."

2 Benjamin, "Catching Our Breath," 148.

3 Franklin, *The Real World of Technology*, 34–35.

4 Benjamin, *Race after Technology*, 114.

5 Wikipedia does a wonderful job of explaining ethical alignment in Dungeons and Dragons: "Alignment is a categorization of the ethical and moral perspective of player characters, non-player characters, and creatures." The categorizations have become a popular meme on the internet and are cultural shorthand for describing characters or players in popular culture. The categories are, Lawful good, Neutral good, Chaotic good, Lawful neutral, (True) neutral, Chaotic neutral, Lawful evil, Neutral evil, Chaotic evil. Wikipedia, s.v. "Alignment (Dungeons & Dragons)," accessed September 27, 2002, https://en.wikipedia.org/wiki/Alignment_(Dungeons_%26_Dragons).

6 Noble, *Algorithms of Oppression*.

7 This quote and more information about the project can be found at "Becoming Homeless: A Human Experience," Virtual Human Interaction Lab, Stanford University, 2020, http://vhil.stanford.edu/becominghomeless/.

8 Hartman, *Scenes of Subjection*, 18.

9 Van Loon et al., "Virtual Reality Perspective-Taking," 15.

10 Innis, *The Bias of Communication*, 33.

11 Chris Milk, "The Future of Virtual Reality," *Medium*, June 16, 2016, https://medium.com/@Within/welcome-to-within-c7d3daba2b55. This blog post has many quotes that are exceptional about the state of VR by a prominent founder in addition to this one. For instance, the top highlight is "Suddenly the challenge is no longer suspending our disbelief—but remembering that what we're experiencing isn't real." It is worth the read.

12 Benjamin, *Race after Technology*, 113.

13 Carey and Quirk, "The Mythos of the Electronic Revolution," 422.

14 Carey and Quirk, "The Mythos of the Electronic Revolution," 396.

15 Atanasoski and Vora, *Surrogate Humanity*, 4.

16 The "firehose" is the term used for large amount of data collected from social media and other digital information companies that is sold to others. Due to the quantity of data, it requires a large amount of processing power, and access is sold at a premium.

17   Stearn, *McLuhan*, 130.

18   Ellul, *The Technological Society.*

19   Weber, *Peasants into Frenchmen.*

20   Virilio, *Original Accident.*

21   Manna, "The Correctness of Nondeterministic Programs," 1.

22   Noble, *Algorithms of Oppression.*

23   Manovich, "Cultural Analytics."

24   Ciccariello-Maher, *Decolonizing Dialectics*, 70.

25   Fanon, *Wretched of the Earth*, 2.

26   Mignolo and Walsh, *On Decoloniality*, 146.

27   Benjamin, "Catching Our Breath."

28   Angwin, Larson, Mattau, et al., "Machine Bias."

29   "Deep Empathy," MIT Media Lab, December 2017–May 2018, accessed November 5, 2022, https://www.media.mit.edu/projects/deep-empathy /overview/.

30   The main menu of the website has an item called "Teach AI," when you click through, you are taken to a page called "survey" (http://deepempathy .mit.edu/survey), a term that comes with its own baggage and positionality between the proctor and survey taker.

31   Vatsyanan, *Man in Technological Society*, 7.

32   Innis, *Changing Concepts of Time.*

33   "Deep Empathy" home page, accessed on November 6, 2022, https:// deepempathy.mit.edu/.

34   McLuhan's "*Playboy* Interview" is filled with racist assumptions regarding a propensity for violence by Indigenous and Black populations, especially under the influence of drugs. However, it is one of the few articles that articulates the relationship between mechanical advancement and genocide for Black and Indigenous populations in the Americas due to the embed-ded ideologies of inferiority of some over others. "The aspiration of our time for wholeness, empathy, and depth of awareness is a natural adjunct of electric technology. The age of mechanical and industry that preceded us found vehement assertion of private outlook the natural mode of expres-sion. Every age has its favorite model of perception and knowledge that is inclined to prescribe for everybody and everything." (McLuhan, "Under-standing Media," 150).

35   McLuhan and Papanek, *Verbio-Voco-Visual Explorations*, Item 14. Please note, in lieu of page numbers, this book is organized by item number.

36   McLuhan and Papanek, *Verbio-Voco-Visual Explorations*, Item 14.

37   Bikolabs, "Empathizing with AI's Psyche," accessed September 27, 2022, https://bikolabs.biko2.com/empathizingwithais/. Bikolabs's website (https:// bikolabs.biko2.com/) provides information on their critical approach to thinking about technology and our future with it.

38 Bikolabs, "Empathizing with AI's Psyche." This was shared with me by Yvonne Lam @yvonnezlam on Twitter.

39 Bikolabs, "Empathizing with AI's Psyche."

40 In 2010, Gizmodo published an article titled "Why I Stalk a Sexy Black Woman on Twitter (And Why You Should, Too)." In the article, a white male writer discusses a Black woman he randomly decided to follow and how he understands her life. In addition to the sexual violence implications of stalking, the article showed a lack of nuance in understanding the woman as fully human, and instead leaned heavily into the Madonna-whore complex. It starts with: "It all started one day when Anil Dash pointed out how many black people use Twitter. I realized most of my Twitter friends are like me: white dorks. So I picked out my new friend and started to pay attention. She's a Christian, but isn't afraid of sex." In addition to this article, at the time there were many calls for non-Black people to follow Black people on twitter to get better insight into Black people without actually engaging them in meaningful interactions. Joel Johnson, "Why I Stalk a Sexy Black Woman on Twitter (And Why You Should, Too)," Gizmodo, July 14, 2010, https://gizmodo.com/why-i-stalk-a-sexy-black-woman-on-twitter-and-why-you-5586970.

41 Chun, "Introduction: Race and/as Technology."

42 Sutherland, "Making a Killing."

43 Dell, "Debunking Digital Twin Technology with Jason Shepherd, CTO of IoT and Edge Computing, Dell Technologies," accessed September 27, 2022, https://www.delltechnologies.com/fi-fi/video-collateral/debunking-digital-twin-technology-with-jason-shepherd-cto-of-iot-and-edge-computing-dell-technologies.htm.

44 Rebecca Koenig, "With Money from Facebook, 10 Colleges Turn Their Campuses into 'Metaversities,'" EdSurge, June 1, 2022, https://www.edsurge.com/news/2022-06-01-with-money-from-facebook-10-colleges-turn-their-campuses-into-metaversities.

45 James Cook, "VR Company Engage Partners with Victory XR to Launch Ten Metaversities in the US," Business Leader, April 7, 2022, https://www.businessleader.co.uk/vr-company-engage-partners-with-victory-xr-to-launch-ten-metaversities-in-the-us/.

46 The VR film production studio VRSE released a VR (9:53) documentary in partnership with the United Nations and Vice titled Waves of Grace, which was part of a larger campaign producing VR films on international crises. The UN website describes the film as follows: "Waves of Grace captures a young woman's tale of love, loss, and rebirth amid the Ebola epidemic. In the film we accompany Decontee Davis, a native of West Point, Liberia, as she guides us through the streets of her township, into schools, hospitals, abandoned buildings and burial grounds. She finds solace by using her immunity to help patients, care for those orphaned, fight stigma, in the faith

of forgiveness." https://unvr.sdgactioncampaign.org/wavesofgrace/. The video is viewable online at https://youtu.be/olwG6MfGvwI.

47 These laws are inspired by the laws of media introduced in Logan and McLuhann, *The Future of the Library*.

Some end thoughts.

1 I have a zine titled "Empathy Is an Ideology: Or, Who Is Culturally Pathologized by the Ideology We Call Empathy," which is available to print from http://jadedid.com/blog/2019/11/13/empathy-is-an-ideology-or-who-is -culturally-pathologized-by-the-ideology-we-call-empathy/.

2 Forgacs, *The Gramsci Reader*, 199.

3 Marx and Engels, *Ruling Class and Ruling Ideals*, 9.

4 Huntington Jr. and Wangchen, *The Emptiness of Emptiness*, 167.

5 Fanon, *Black Skin, White Masks*, 82.

6 Quellel, "Franz Fanon and Colonized Man," 11.

7 Stein, *On the Problem of Empathy*, 69.

8 Mutual recognition requires engagement from both sides. This will fail. The failure of mutual recognition leads to compassion. Compassion, above all else, allows for a one-sided recognition and allows for the moments of mutual recognition to be a surprise.

Bibliography.

Ahmed, Sara. *The Cultural Politics of Emotion.* Edinburgh: Edinburgh University Press, 2014.

Ahmed, Sara. *Willful Subjects.* Durham, NC: Duke University Press, 2014.

Angwin, Julia, Jeff Larson, Surya Mattau, and Lauren Kirchner. "Machine Bias." *ProPublica,* May 23, 2016. https://www.propublica.org/article/machine-bias-risk -assessments-in-criminal-sentencing.

Arora, Gabo, and Chris Milk, dirs. *Waves of Grace.* Hollywood: VRSE.works, 2015.

Arora, Gabo, and Barry Pousman, dirs. *Clouds over Sidra.* Hollywood: VRSE.works, 2015.

Assmann, Aleida, and Ines Detmers, eds. *Empathy and Its Limits.* New York: Springer, 2015.

Atanasoski, Neda, and Kalindi Vora. *Surrogate Humanity: Race, Robots, and the Politics of Technological Futures.* Durham, NC: Duke University Press, 2019.

Augé, Marc, ed. *La communauté illusoire.* Paris: Payot and Rivages, 2010.

Augé, Marc. *Oblivion.* Minneapolis: University of Minnesota Press, 2004.

Bakhtin, Mikhail Mikhaïlovich. *Toward a Philosophy of the Act.* Austin: University of Texas Press, 2010.

Balme, Christopher B. *Pacific Performances: Theatricality and Cross-Cultural Encounter in the South Seas.* Basingstoke: Palgrave Macmillan, 2007.

Balme, Christopher B. "Staging the Pacific: Framing Authenticity in Performances for Tourists at the Polynesian Cultural Center." *Theatre Journal* 50, no. 1 (1998): 53–70.

Bancel, Nicolas, Pascal Blanchard, Gilles Boëtsch, Eric Deroo, and Sandrine Lemaire. *Zoos humains: De la Vénus hottentote aux reality shows.* Paris: Éditions La Decouverte, 2002.

Baron-Cohen, Simon, Michael Lombado, and Helen Tager-Flusberg, eds. *Understanding Other Minds: Perspectives from Developmental Cognitive Neuroscience.* Oxford, UK: Oxford University Press, 2000.

Batson, C. Daniel. "These Things Called Empathy: Eight Related but Distinct Phenomena." In *The Social Neuroscience of Empathy*, edited by Jean Decety and William John Ickes, 3–16. Cambridge, MA: MIT Press, 2009.

Bein, Steve. *Compassion and Moral Guidance*. Honolulu: University of Hawai'i Press, 2013.

Benjamin, Ruha. "Catching Our Breath: Critical Race STS and the Carceral Imagination." *Engaging Science, Technology, and Society* 2 (2016): 145–56.

Benjamin, Ruha. *Race after Technology: Abolitionist Tools for the New Jim Code*. Cambridge, UK: Polity, 2019.

Bentley, Tom. *Empires of Remorse: Narrative, Postcolonialism and Apologies for Colonial Atrocity*. New York: Routledge, 2015.

Berger, John. "From *Ways of Seeing*." In *The Feminism and Visual Culture Reader*, edited by Amelia Jones, 37–39. London: Routledge, 2003.

Bergner, Gwen S. *Taboo Subjects: Race, Sex, and Psychoanalysis*. Minneapolis: University of Minnesota Press, 2005.

Bergson, Henri. *Matter and Memory*. Translated by Nancy Margaret Paul and W. Scott Palmer. Mineola, NY: Dover, 2004.

Bikolabs. "Empathizing with AI's Psyche." https://bikolabs.biko2.com/empathizing-withais/, last accessed February 24, 2023.

Blanchard, Pascal, Gilles Boetsch, and Nanette Jacomijn Snoep. *Human Zoos: The Invention of the Savage*. Arles: Actes Sud, 2011.

Bloom, Paul. *Against Empathy: The Case for Rational Compassion*. New York: Ecco, 2018.

Bohart, Arthur C., and Leslie S. Greenberg. *Empathy Reconsidered: New Directions in Psychotherapy*. Washington, DC: American Psychological Association, 1997.

Breittmayer, Albert. "Rapport sur Congrès de Bourg en 1888." *Bulletin de la Société de géographie de Lyon* 8 (1889): 119–31. https://gallica.bnf.fr/ark:/12148/bpt6k5667304z/f119.item.

Brennan, Teresa. *The Transmission of Affect*. Ithaca, NY: Cornell University Press, 2004.

Campbell, Joseph Keim, Michael O'Rourke, and Harry S. Silverstein, eds. *Time and Identity*. Cambridge, MA: MIT Press, 2010.

Campt, Tina M. *Listening to Images*. Durham, NC: Duke University Press, 2017.

Carey, James W., and John J. Quirk. "The Mythos of the Electronic Revolution." *American Scholar* (1970): 395–424.

Carr, David. *Phenomenology and the Problem of History*. Evanston, IL: Northwestern University Press, 1974.

Caswell, Michelle, and Marika Cifor. "From Human Rights to Feminist Ethics: Radical Empathy in the Archives." *Archivaria* 81, no. 1 (2016): 23–43.

Chamayou, Grégoire. *Manhunts: A Philosophical History*. Princeton, NJ: Princeton University Press, 2012.

Chun, Wendy Hui Kyong. "Introduction: Race and/as Technology; or, How to Do Things to Race." *Camera Obscura* 24, no. 1(70) (2009): 7–35. https://doi.org/10.1215/02705346-2008-013.

Chun, Wendy Hui Kyong. "Race and/as Technology; or, How to Do Things to Race." In *Race after the Internet*, edited by Lisa Nakamura and Peter A. Chow-White, 44–66. New York: Routledge, 2013.

Ciccariello-Maher, George. *Decolonizing Dialectics*. Durham, NC: Duke University Press, 2017.

Cmiel, Kenneth, and John Durham Peters. *Promiscuous Knowledge: Information, Image, and Other Truth Games in History*. Chicago: University of Chicago Press, 2020.

Coles, Prophecy. *The Uninvited Guest from the Unremembered Past: An Exploration of the Unconscious Transmission of Trauma across the Generations*. New York: Routledge, 2018.

Davoine, Françoise, and Jean-Max Gaudillière. *History beyond Trauma: Whereof One Cannot Speak, Thereof One Cannot Stay Silent*. New York: Other Press, 2004.

Decety, Jean, and Sara D. Hodges. "The Social Neuroscience of Empathy." In *Bridging Social Psychology: Benefits of Transdisciplinary Approaches*, edited by Paul A. M. Van Lange, 103–9. New York: Routledge, 2006.

Delmare, Georges "Chez les Hottentots." *Gil Blas*, July 21, 1888. https://gallica.bnf.fr /ark:/12148/bpt6k2318721.

Dixon, Joan Broadhurst, and Eric Cassidy, eds. *Virtual Futures: Cyberotics, Technology and Posthuman Pragmatism*. New York: Routledge, 2005.

Ellul, Jacques. *The Technological Society*. Translated by John Wilkinson. New York: Vintage Books, 1964.

Ernst, Wolfgang. *Digital Memory and the Archive*. Minneapolis: University of Minnesota Press, 2013.

Fanon, Frantz. *Black Skin, White Masks*. Translated by Charles Lam Markmann. New York: Grove Press, 2008.

Fanon, Frantz. "The North African Syndrome." Translated by Haakon Chevalier. In *Toward the African Revolution: Political Essays*. New York: Grove Press, 1988.

Fanon, Frantz. *Toward the African Revolution: Political Essays*. Translated by Haakon Chevalier. New York: Grove Press, 1988.

Fanon, Frantz. *The Wretched of the Earth*. Translated by Richard Philcox. New York: Grove Atlantic, 2007.

Fauvelle-Aymar, François-Xavier. *L'invention du Hottentot: Histoire du regard occidental sur les Khoisan, XVe–XIXe siècle*. Paris: Publications de la Sorbonne, 2002.

Forgacs, David. *The Gramsci Reader: Selected Writings 1916–1935*. New York: New York University Press, 2000.

Franklin, Ursula Martius. *The Real World of Technology*. Toronto: House of Anansi, 1999.

Franklin, Ursula Martius. *Ursula Franklin Speaks: Thoughts and Afterthoughts*. Montreal: McGill-Queen's Press, 2014.

Franklin, Ursula Martius. *Will Women Change Technology or Will Technology Change Women?* Ottawa: Canadian Research Institute for the Advancement of Women, 1985.

Fressoz, Jean-Baptiste. *L'apocalypse joyeuse: Une histoire du risque technologique*. Paris: Éditions du Seuil, 2012.

Friesem, Yonty. "Empathy for the Digital Age: Using Video Production to Enhance Social, Emotional, and Cognitive Skills." In *Emotions, Technology, and*

Behaviors, edited by Sharon Y. Tettegah and Doroth L. Espelage, 21–45. Boston: Academic Press, 2016.

Fromm, Gerard, ed. *Lost in Transmission: Studies of Trauma across Generations.* London: Routledge, 2012.

Fusco, Coco, and Brian Wallis, eds. *Only Skin Deep: Changing Visions of the American Self.* New York: Harry N. Abrams, 2003.

Garde-Hansen, Joanne. *Media and Memory.* Edinburgh: Edinburgh University Press, 2011.

Gertz, Nolen. *Nihilism and Technology.* Lanham, MD: Rowman and Littlefield, 2018.

Ginsberg, Morris. *The Idea of Progress: A Revaluation.* London: Methuen, 1953.

Goubert, Liesbet, Kenneth D. Craig, and Ann Buysse. "Perceiving Others in Pain: Experimental and Clinical Evidence on the Role of Empathy." In *The Social Neuroscience of Empathy*, edited by Jean Decety and William Ickes, 153–65. Cambridge, MA: MIT Press, 2011.

Grau, Oliver. *Virtual Art: From Illusion to Immersion.* Cambridge, MA: MIT Press, 2003.

Greenberg, Jay. *Object Relations in Psychoanalytic Theory.* Cambridge, MA: Harvard University Press, 1983.

Hagenbeck, Carl. *Beasts and Men: Being Carl Hagenbeck's Experiences for Half a Century among Wild Animals.* London: Longmans, Green, 1909.

Halbwachs, Maurice. *La mémoire collective.* Paris: Albin Michel, 1997.

Hartman, Saidiya V. *Scenes of Subjection: Terror, Slavery, and Self-Making in Nineteenth-Century America.* New York: Oxford University Press, 1997.

Hartman, Saidiya V. *Wayward Lives, Beautiful Experiments: Intimate Histories of Social Upheaval.* New York: W. W. Norton, 2019.

Hartshorn, Leon Roundy. "Mormon Education in the Bold Years." EdD thesis, Stanford University, 1965.

Heim, Otto, and Caroline Wiedmer. *Inventing the Past: Memory Work in Culture and History.* Basel: Schwabe Verlag, 2005.

Hogan, Robert. "Development of an Empathy Scale." *Journal of Consulting and Clinical Psychology* 33, no. 3 (1969): 307–16. https://doi.org/10.1037/h0027580.

Hume, David. *A Treatise of Human Nature.* Oxford, UK: Clarendon Press, 1896.

Huntington, Clair W., Jr., and Namgyal Wangchen. *The Emptiness of Emptiness: An Introduction to Early Indian Madhyamika.* Honolulu: University of Hawai'i Press, 1995.

Hurston, Zora Neale. "How It Feels to Be Colored Me" (1928). In *Worlds of Difference: Inequality in the Aging Experience*, 95–97. Newbury Park, CA: Pine Forge Press, 2000.

Huzar, Eugène. *La fin du monde par la science.* Paris: Librairie de E. Dentu, 1858.

Ihde, Don. *Existential Technics.* Albany, NY: SUNY Press, 1983.

Innis, Harold Adams. *Changing Concepts of Time.* Lanham, MD: Rowman and Littlefield, 2004.

Innis, Harold Adams. *The Bias of Communication.* Toronto: University of Toronto Press, 2008.

Jahoda, Gustav. "Theodor Lipps and the Shift from 'Sympathy' to 'Empathy.'" *Journal of the History of the Behavioral Sciences* 41, no. 2 (2005): 151–63.

Katz, Robert L. *Empathy: Its Nature and Uses*. New York: Collier-Macmillan, 1964.

Lanzoni, Susan. *Empathy: A History*. New Haven, CT: Yale University Press, 2018.

Lefebvre, Bernard. *Avec de Gaulle en Afrique*. Luneray: Bertout, 1990.

Le Goff, Jacques. *History and Memory*. New York: Columbia University Press, 1992.

Lembezat, Bertrand. *Palabres En Pays Kirdi: Itinéraire D'un Jeaune Administrateur Au Nord Cameroun 1938–1940*. Paris: Harmattan, https://archives.org/details /palabresenpayskioooolemb, 2009.

Lembezat, Bertrand. *La colonne, Ou, Journal D'un Mercenaire Hétéroclite*. Paris: Marsouins et méharistes, 2008.

Lembezat, Bertrand. *Les populations païennes du Nord-Cameroun et de l'Adamaoua*. Paris: Presses Universitaires de France, 1961.

Lembezat, Bertrand. *Le Cameroun*. 3rd ed. Paris: Éditions maritimes et coloniales, 1961.

Lembezat, Bertrand. *Mukulehe: Un clan montagnard du Nord-Ca meroun; coutumes, rites, croyances. Avec 12 croquis, 1 carte et 108 photos de l'auteur*. Paris: Berger-Levrault, 1952.

Lembezat, Bertrand, and Robert Carmet. *Eve Noire*. Neuchatel: Éditions Ides et calendes, 1952.

Lembezat, Bertrand, and Institut français d'Afrique noire. *Kirdi Les Populations Païennes Du Nord-Cameroun*. Douala: IFAN, 1950.

Le Roux, Hugues. "La vie à Paris." *Le Temps*, August 18, 1888. https://gallica.bnf.fr. ark:.12148/bpt6k2318721.

Le Roy, Edmond. "Les Hottentots à Paris." *Le Gaulois: Littéraire et Politique*, July 22, 1888.

Lieberman, Matthew D. "The Neural Correlates of Empathy: Experience, Automaticity, and Prosocial Behavior." *Journal of Cognitive Neuroscience* 24, no. 1 (2012): 235–45.

Lipps, Theodor. "Einfühlung, innere Nachahmung und Organenempfindungen." *Revue Philosophique FranceFrance et de l'Etranger* 56 (1903): 660–61.

Logan, Robert K., and Marshall McLuhan. *The Future of the Library: From Electric Media to Digital Media*. New York: Peter Lang, 2016.

Lorde, Audre. "Learning from the 60s." In *Sister Outsider: Essays and Speeches*, 134–44. Berkeley, CA: Crossing Press, 1984.

Lorde, Audre. *Sister Outsider: Essays and Speeches*. New York: Penguin Classics, 2020.

Lux, Vanessa, and Sigrid Weigel, eds. *Empathy: Epistemic Problems and Cultural-Historical Perspectives of a Cross-Disciplinary Concept*. New York: Springer, 2017.

Magrì, Elisa, and Dermot Moran. *Empathy, Sociality, and Personhood: Essays on Edith Stein's Phenomenological Investigations*. New York: Springer, 2017.

Maibom, Heidi Lene, ed. *Empathy and Morality*. New York: Oxford University Press, 2014.

Manna, Zohar. "The Correctness of Nondeterministic Programs." *Artificial Intelligence* 1, nos. 1–2 (1970): 1–26.

Manovich, Lev. "Cultural Analytics: Visualising Cultural Patterns in the Era of 'More Media.'" *Domus* (Spring 2009).

Manovich, Lev. *The Language of New Media*. Cambridge, MA: MIT Press, 2002.

Marien, Mary Warner. *Photography: A Cultural History*. London: Laurence King Publishing, 2006.

Marx, Karl, and Friedrich Engels. *The Ruling Class and the Ruling Ideas* (1845). In *Media and Cultural Studies: Keyworks*, edited by Meenakshi Gigi Durham and Douglas Kellner, 9–12. Malden, MA: Wiley-Blackwell, 2012.

Matravers, Derek. 1998. *Art and Emotion*. New York: Oxford University Press.

Matravers, Derek. *Empathy*. Hoboken, NJ: John Wiley and Sons, 2017.

Matravers, Derek. "Empathy and the Danger of Inventing Words." *Philosopher's Magazine* 85, no. 2 (2019): 26–31.

McKittrick, Katherine. "Mathematics Black Life." *Black Scholar* 44, no. 2 (Summer 2014): 16–28.

McLuhan, Marshall. *Media Research: Technology, Art and Communication*. London: Routledge, 2014.

McLuhan, Marshall. "The New Art of Science Which the Electronic or Post-Mechanical Age Has to Invent," item 14. In *Laws of Media: The New Science*, edited by Marshall McLuhan and Eric McLuhan. Toronto: University of Toronto Press, 1992.

McLuhan, Marshall. "*Playboy* Interview: A Candid Conversation with the High Priest of Popcult and Metaphysician of Media." In *Essential McLuhan*, edited by Eric McLuhan and Frank Zingrone, 233–69. New York: Routledge, 1997.

McLuhan, Marshall. "Understanding Media. The Extensions of Man." In *Essential McLuhan*, edited by Eric McLuhan and Frank Zingrone, 149–79. New York: Routledge, 1997.

McLuhan, Marshall, and Eric McLuhan. *Laws of Media: The New Science*. Toronto: University of Toronto Press, 1992.

McLuhan, Marshall, and Victor J. Papanek. *Verbio-Voco-Visual Explorations*. New York: Something Else Press, 1967.

Memmi, Albert. *Decolonization and the Decolonized*. Minneapolis: University of Minnesota Press, 2006.

Meyers, Diana T. *Subjection and Subjectivity: Psychoanalytic Feminism and Moral Philosophy*. London: Routledge, 2014.

Mignolo, Walter D., and Catherine E. Walsh. *On Decoloniality: Concepts, Analytics, Praxis*. Durham, NC: Duke University Press, 2018.

Nakamura, Lisa. "Feeling Good about Feeling Bad: Virtuous Virtual Reality and the Automation of Racial Empathy." *Journal of Visual Culture* 19, no. 1 (2020): 47–64.

Nakamura, Lisa. 2019. "Virtual Reality and the Feeling of Virtue." Keynote address. ACM Digital Library Proceedings of the 2019 On Designing Interactive Systems (DIS 2019) Conference, 3-3. San Diego, CA, June 13–28, 2019. https://doi.org/10.1145/3322276.332420.

Nelems, Rebeccah, and Nic Theo, eds. *Exploring Empathy: Its Propagations, Perimeters and Potentialities*. Leiden: Brill Academic, 2017.

Noble, Safiya Umoja. *Algorithms of Oppression*. New York: New York University Press, 2018.

Oliver, Kelly. *The Colonization of Psychic Space: A Psychoanalytic Social Theory of Oppression*. Minneapolis: University of Minnesota Press, 2004.

Olson, Gary. *Empathy Imperiled: Capitalism, Culture, and the Brain*. New York: Springer, 2013.

Olsson, Andreas, and Victoria Spring. "The Vicarious Brain: Integrating Empathy and Emotional Learning." In *Neuronal Correlates of Empathy: From Rodent to Human*, edited by Ksenia Z. Meyza and Ewelina Knapska, 7–23. Cambridge, MA: Academic Press, 2018.

Oxley, Julinna. *The Moral Dimensions of Empathy: Limits and Applications in Ethical Theory and Practice*. New York: Springer, 2011.

"Par-ci, Par-là." *Le Voleur Illustré: Cabinet de Lecture Universel*, August 2, 1888, 490–91. https://gallica.bnf.fr/ark:/12148/bpt6k62372486/f11.vertical.r=Le%20 Voleur%20Illustr%C3%A9hottentot%20hottentot.

Pedwell, Carolyn. "De-Colonizing Empathy: Thinking Affect Transnationally." *Samyukta: A Journal of Women's Studies* 16, no. 1 (2016): 27–49.

Pedwell, Carolyn. "Mediated Habits: Images, Networked Affect and Social Change." *Subjectivity* 10, no. 2 (2017): 147–69.

Pedwell, Carolyn. "Theorizing 'African' Female Genital Cutting and 'Western' Body Modifications: A Critique of the Continuum and Analogue Approaches." *Feminist Review* 86, no. 1 (2007): 45–66.

Peters, John Durham. *Speaking into the Air: A History of the Idea of Communication*. Chicago: University of Chicago Press, 2012.

Pihlström, Sami. *Transcendental Guilt: Reflections on Ethical Finitude*. Lanham, MD: Lexington Books, 2011.

Ploix, M. "Les Hottentots ou Khoikhoi et leur religion." *Revue d'Anthropologie* (1887): 570–89.

Quellel, Charif. "Franz Fanon and Colonized Man." *Africa Today* 17, no. 1 (1970): 8–11. https://www.jstor.org/stable/4185057.

Ricœur, Paul. *Memory, History, Forgetting*. Chicago: University of Chicago Press, 2004.

Rosenberger, Robert, and Peter-Paul Verbeek. *Postphenomenological Investigations: Essays on Human-Technology Relations*. Lanham, MD: Lexington Books, 2015.

Roth, Michael S. *Memory, Trauma, and History: Essays on Living with the Past*. New York: Columbia University Press, 2012.

Sandau, Jannalee. "Why There Are Tattoos and Strapless Costumes at the Polynesian Cultural Center." LDS Living, February 27, 2019. https://www.ldsliving .com/why-there-are-tattoos-and-strapless-costumes-at-the-polynesian-cultural -center/s/83359.

Scheler, Max. *The Nature of Sympathy*. London: Routledge, 2017.

Sekula, Allan. "The Body and the Archive." *October* 39 (1986): 3–64.

Sekula, Allan. "The Traffic in Photographs." *Art Journal* 41, no. 1 (1981): 15–25.

Sharpe, Christina. *Monstrous Intimacies: Making Post-Slavery Subjects*. Durham, NC: Duke University Press, 2009.

Singer, Tania, and Claus Lamm. "The Social Neuroscience of Empathy." *Annals of the New York Academy of Sciences* 1156, no. 1 (2009): 81–96.

Spencer, Craig. "Having and Fighting Ebola: Public Health Lessons from a Clinician Turned Patient." *New England Journal of Medicine* 372, no. 12 (2015): 1089–91.

Stearn, Gerald Emanuel. *McLuhan: Hot and Cool*. New York: Dial Press, 1967.

Stein, Edith. *On the Problem of Empathy*, 3rd ed. Washington, DC: ICS Publications, 1989.

Sutherland, Tonia. "Making a Killing: On Race, Ritual, and (Re)membering in Digital Culture." *Preservation, Digital Technology and Culture* 46, no. 1 (2017): 32–40.

Thode-Arora, Hilke, ed. *From Samoa with Love? Retracing the Footsteps.* Munich: Hirmer, 2014.

Topinard, Paul. "La stéatopygie des Hottentotes du Jardin d'acclimatation." *Revue d'Anthropologie* (1889): 194–99. https://gallica.bnf.fr/ark:/12148/bpt6k1045317/f2.item.

Trézenem, Édouard, and Bertrand Lembezat. *La France Équatoriale: L'afrique Équatoriale Française.* Paris: Société d'éditions géographiques maritimes et colonialen, 1947.

Truscott, Ross. "Empathy's Echo: Post-Apartheid Fellow Feeling." *Safundi* 17, no. 2 (2016): 249–69.

Tsing, Anna Lowenhaupt. "On Nonscalability: The Living World Is Not Amenable to Precision-Nested Scales." *Common Knowledge* 18, no. 3 (2012): 505–24.

Ulrikab, Abraham. *The Diary of Abraham Ulrikab: Text and Context.* Edited and translated by Hartmut Lutz. Ottawa: University of Ottawa Press, 2005. https://archive.org/details/diaryofabrahamulooooulri.

Van Loon, Austin, Jeremy Bailenson, Jamille Zaki, Joshua Bostick, and Robb Willer. "Virtual Reality Perspective-Taking Increases Cognitive Empathy for Specific Others." *PloS One* 13, no. 8 (2018). https://doi.org/10.1372/journal.pone.0202442.

Vatsyayan, Sachchidananda. *Man in Technological Society: M. N. Roy Memorial Lecture.* Dehradun: Indian Renaissance Institute; New Delhi: Indian Radical Humanist Association, 1983.

Verbeek, Peter-Paul. *Moralizing Technology: Understanding and Designing the Morality of Things.* Chicago: University of Chicago Press, 2011.

Virilio, Paul. *The Original Accident.* Cambridge, UK: Polity, 2007.

Virilio, Paul. *Speed and Politics.* Los Angeles: Semiotext(e), 2006.

Vischer, Robert, Harry Francis Mallgrave, and Eleftherios Ikonomou. *Empathy, Form, and Space: Problems in German Aesthetics, 1873–1893.* Chicago: University of Chicago Press, 1994.

Wade, Lisa. "Human Zoos at the Turn of the 20th Century." *Sociological Images,* October 15, 2012. https://thesocietypages.org/socimages/2012/10/15/human-zoos-at-the-turn-of-the-20th-century/.

Wallis, Brian. "Black Bodies, White Science: Louis Agassiz's Slave Daguerreotypes." *American Art* 9, no. 2 (Summer 1995): 38–61. https://www.jstor.org/stable/3109184.

Warren, Calvin L. *Ontological Terror: Blackness, Nihilism, and Emancipation.* Durham, NC: Duke University Press, 2018.

Weber, Eugen. *Peasants into Frenchmen: The Modernization of Rural France, 1870–1914.* Redwood City, CA: Stanford University Press, 1976.

Willis, Deborah, and Carla Williams. *The Black Female Body: A Photographic History.* Philadelphia: Temple University Press; London: Eurospan, 2002.

Winnicott, Donald W. *The Maturational Processes and the Facilitating Environment: Studies in the Theory of Emotional Development.* London: Routledge, 2018.

Young, Harvey. *Embodying Black Experience: Stillness, Critical Memory, and the Black Body.* Ann Arbor: University of Michigan Press, 2010.

Me, myself, and you: A biography.

In lieu of a traditional biography in which I share my credentials, expertise, and accomplishments, I would like to offer the following composites of many first conversations that have taken place in my life.

> **At Home:** Hello, Black Girl. I get you. I am the first in my family, too. There is an assumption that we can connect because we are in time together. The first to make it to the middle class. The first to be educated. The first to break away from the cycle of suffering that is imagined for the poor and the marginalized, especially marginalized people of color. We aren't so different. Together we will be the first to escape into the common time of progress.
>
> **Abroad:** It is so horrible how they treat your people back there. As you can see here, in Country X, we do not have the same racism, but please do ignore that the only places we allow our citizens who look like you or allow your ancestors to exist in are here in *e, f,* and *g.* But we do want them to be ever so successful, and at least we do not treat them like you are treated where you are from. They are our citizens, after all. You are second class at home.

I am a Western woman who occupies the unique position that often took hold in settler-slave colonies. I am of mixed heritage, even though I am unapologetically Black. My experience serves as an empty signifier of slavery while also destroying the myth that there is a radical coming together that will lessen the psychic blows of racism, colonization, and oppression. My professional success comes with a unique encounter, a false assumption of my specialness due to my achievements. The assumed experience (first generation, first doctor, who grew up in abject poverty in one of those places where Black people live) is false. I've worked at the university where the Blackest of my great-grandparents met (Columbia). I currently work at another university (University of Pennsylvania), down the street from the affluent suburb where my great-grandmother was born. There is a rumor in an obituary that she attended here before she attended Columbia. I am in the third generation of my family that has some form of doctor. I often half-joke that I am the underachiever in my family because of the type of doctor I became. My grandfather is a doctor of dental surgery, and my aunt a doctor of medicine. I, on the other hand, studied French language for my BA and French history and culture before turning to communication studies to focus on digital media, culture, and performance studies. I grew up in an affluent white community. And so, white man and woman, or other person who is not me, you cannot empathize with me. I break the expectations too often.

On the other hand, the experience of being Other in America is one of forced empathy. I am and am not this thing at any given time, because this thing that is belonging is dependent on my ability to navigate through and find my place in a white supremacist society. That is to say, even the term "American" in the United States signifies whiteness above all else. Even outside of this place, when I am in other countries, my experience comes predefined. As a Black American (Western) woman, I am not allowed to move freely through the world, taking on the experiences of others and letting them go as is convenient. As part of this motley crew of a global Black and African diaspora, I share all of their stories, if not consciously, then as experiences put upon me as I move from place to place.

Index.

Sutherland, Tonia, 88
sympathy, 3,4
Syria, *see* "Deep Empathy"

technoliberalism, 73
Le Temps (Paris), 47
Thege, Mr., 47, 50–51
trigger warning, 30–31, 33, 36–37
Truscott, Ross, 8, 31
Tuffery, Michel, 17
Tui Ātua Tupua Tamasese Efi, 16

Ulrikab, Abraham, 27–28
UNICEF, 80, 83

"La vie à Paris," 47–51
virtual reality, 6–7, 13, 65–71, 73, 89–91
"Virtual Reality Perspective-Taking Increases
   Cognitive Empathy for Specific Others," 70
*Le Voleur Illustré: Cabinet de Lecture
   Universel*, 53
Vora, Kalindi, 73
VRSE, *see* "Within"

Wallis, Bryan, 25
Walsh, Catherine, 26
Wangchen, Namgyal, 95
Within (VRSE), 71
The Wretched of the Earth, 78

www.ingramcontent.com/pod-product-compliance
Lightning Source LLC
Chambersburg PA
CBHW050655270326
41927CB00012B/3033